THE SKYE TRAIL

About the Authors

Paul and Helen Webster have a lifelong passion for walking and exploring the outdoors. In 2003–4 they undertook a 4000-mile continuous backpack across Europe, an experience which left them believing that travelling on foot allows you to see things and meet people that might otherwise be overlooked.

While living on the Isle of Skye, Paul and Helen established Walkhighlands, a free interactive online guide to walking in Scotland, and have been lucky enough to be able to spend as much time as possible exploring the whole of Scotland on two feet.

Paul and Helen have written 11 walking books about Scotland, including a guide to the Munros, and they are both actively involved in various conservation and tourism organisations, including the John Muir Trust and the Mountaineering Council of Scotland.

THE SKYE TRAIL

by Paul and Helen Webster

CICERONE

2 POLICE SQUARE, MILNTHORPE, CUMBRIA LA7 7PY
www.cicerone.co.uk

Printed by KHL Printing, Singapore
A catalogue record for this book is available from the British Library.
All photographs are by the authors unless otherwise stated.

Acknowledgments

We would like to acknowledge the following people for their help in the researching and writing of this guidebook: Donald Kennedy, Highland Council; John Phillips, Highland Council; Bryan Clark of Simply Scotland Tours; Sylvia Porter; and Rob and Hayley Blake.

Advice to Readers

While every effort is made by our authors to ensure the accuracy of guidebooks as they go to print, changes can occur during the lifetime of an edition. If we know of any, there will be an Updates tab on this book's page on the Cicerone website (www.cicerone.co.uk), so please check before planning your trip. We also advise that you check information about such things as transport, accommodation and shops locally. Even rights of way can be altered over time. We are always grateful for information about any discrepancies between a guidebook and the facts on the ground, sent by email to info@cicerone.co.uk or by post to Cicerone, 2 Police Square, Milnthorpe LA7 7PY, United Kingdom.

Front cover: Cathedral Rock (Stage 2)

CONTENTS

Jerusalem, Athens and Rome,
I would see them before I die.
But I'd rather not see any one of the three
than be exiled for ever from Skye.
What are the wonders there,
Stranger doth ask of me?
What is there not? I reply like a Scot,
For him that hath eyes to see.
Lovest thou mountains great,
Peaks to the clouds that soar,
Corrie and fell where eagles dwell,
And cataracts rush evermore?
Lovest thou green grassy glades,
By the sunshine sweetly kist,
Murmuring waves and echoing caves?
Then go to the Isle of Mist.

From Alexander Nicolson's The Isle of Skye, 1862

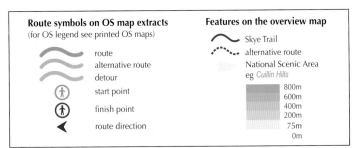

Route symbols on OS map extracts
(for OS legend see printed OS maps)

route
alternative route
detour
start point
finish point
route direction

Features on the overview map

Skye Trail
alternative route
National Scenic Area
eg *Cuillin Hills*

800m
600m
400m
200m
75m
0m

Warning

Mountain walking can be a dangerous activity carrying a risk of personal injury or death. It should be undertaken only by those with a full understanding of the risks and with the training and experience to evaluate them. While every care and effort has been taken in the preparation of this guide, the user should be aware that conditions can be highly variable and can change quickly, materially affecting the seriousness of a mountain walk. Therefore, except for any liability which cannot be excluded by law, neither Cicerone nor the authors accept liability for damage of any nature (including damage to property, personal injury or death) arising directly or indirectly from the information in this book.

To call out the Mountain Rescue, ring 999 or the international emergency number 112: this will connect you via any available network. Once connected to the emergency operator, ask for the police.

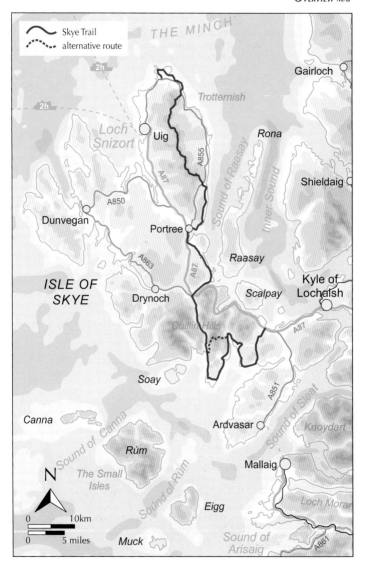

Sheep at Camas Malag (Stage 7) with the peak of Bla Bheinn in the background on the final stage of the Trail from Torrin to Broadford

INTRODUCTION

Start of shoreline path to Sligachan (Stage 4)

The Isle of Skye holds a special place in many people's hearts. Its romantic history, majestic mountains, stunning coastline and the Gaelic language and culture all draw people back time and time again. Many rush around the best known sights of the island in a few days, but for those who wish to experience Skye properly, there can be few better ways than by tackling a long-distance walk. A multi-day trek forces us to see the landscapes we pass through in a more complete way. The long-distance walker soon gets into a rhythm of walking each day then heading for food and shelter, and has time to discover the people, wildlife and history in a landscape, as well as absorbing its physical beauty.

The Skye Trail is an unofficial route snaking from the northern tip of the island and extending to Broadford in the south. It offers a unique opportunity to tap into the real spirit of the island on foot. It should be said that walking this 'trail' is nothing like the West Highland Way or other formal routes. There are no signs and there is not even a path for some of the way. Self-reliance, fitness and good navigational skills will all be called upon. Whether making use of island hospitality or opting for the freedom of a tent, completing the continuous route represents a real challenge and a fitting match for the epic landscapes found on Skye.

The trail begins with a spectacular and relatively undiscovered coastal section before taking to the Trotternish Ridge – regarded by many as among the very finest ridgewalks in the UK. After another coastal section the route takes in the picturesque capital of Skye – Portree – before running through the sheltered Braes district. Soon the route continues in the shadow of the mighty Cuillin – the most Alpine mountains in the UK – to reach Elgol, celebrated for its view across Loch Scavaig. There follows an atmospheric section through two deserted villages – a reminder of the Highland Clearances and the darker side of the island's history – before arrival at Broadford and journey's end. The route has been designed so that, with some careful planning, it is possible to have somewhere to stay each night; but it also makes a superb backpacking expedition with plenty of opportunities for wild camping as well as the option of a couple of campsites and a bothy.

The original idea for a backpacking route on the island came from photographer David Paterson's book *A Long Walk on the Isle of Skye* published back in 1999. Paterson's route was from south to north but included what many felt to be a disappointing first stage with a good deal of bog-hopping or roadwalking. Since then the idea has been taken up by others,

including Cameron McNeish who made a BBC TV programme – accompanied by an inspirational coffee-table book – about the route, starting from the northern end of the island and finishing at Broadford. In the same year the walkers' website www.walkhighlands.co.uk – run by the authors of this guide – published an online guide to the trail, refining and improving upon the routes detailed previously. The Highland Council's Ranger Service began walking sections of the trail as individual day walks, and now this detailed guidebook is the first designed to be taken along as a guide on the trail itself.

EARLY HISTORY

The Isle of Skye has long drawn people to its green and relatively mild shores, with evidence of the first settlements – such as a shell midden near Staffin – dating back 5000 years. At the High Pasture Cave system near Broadford archaeologists continue to unearth evidence of an important ceremonial destination from the Bronze Age. There are a number of Bronze and Iron Age forts and other remains on the island, one of which, Dun Ringill, can be visited on a short detour from Stage 6 of the Skye Trail, between Elgol and Torrin.

The name of the starting point for the Skye Trail, Rubha Hunish (pronounced 'rooa hoonish'), reflects the long history of Norse influence, *Hunish* coming from the Norse meaning

Looking back to the cliffs of Rubha Hunish from the northernmost point of Skye (Stage 1)

headland of the bear cub, while *Rubha* is Gaelic for headland and tells of what became the dominant cultural strand here. Many Skye names remain influenced by the long period of Norse rule which lasted from the 9th century to 11th century; the Norse referred to the island as Skuy, meaning misty isle and probably the root of the name Skye. The Gaelic translation of this – Eilean a' Cheò – is still often seen today, although the original Gaelic name for the island is An t-Eilean Sgitheanach – the Winged Isle.

For many centuries Skye was loosely controlled as part of the Lordship of the Isles, which covered much of the far west part of the Scottish mainland as well as most of the Hebrides. Sometimes falling under Norwegian control, the Lords depended on control of the seas for their power, and a network of forts and castles were built close to the sea during this period. The seizure of power by Somerled and his ensuing dynasty was the start of the true rule of the Lord of the Isles, with power and allegiances shifting a number of times, for example when Angus Òg was given the Lordship as a reward for supporting Robert the Bruce. The Lordship was, however, almost independent from the rest of Scotland, so much so that in 1462 the reigning Lord, John MacDonald II, made a pact with Edward IV of England to overthrow the Scottish crown. His treachery was to cost the MacDonalds their lands, which were passed to James IV of Scotland; the Hebrides including Skye were at last brought under the control of the Scottish crown.

Cliffs of Leac nan Forcan in winter (Stage 2)

THE MACDONALDS AND THE MACLEODS

Clan warfare dominated the later period of the Lordship of the Isles and during this time the Isle of Skye was dominated by two great clans, the MacDonalds and the MacLeods. The rivalry between the two led to bloodshed and violence across the island during several centuries. Leod, the founder of Clan MacLeod (clan simply means children), was one of the sons of King Olav the Black, the last King of the Isle of Man and the Western Isles who was defeated by Somerled. The MacLeod seat was at Dunvegan from a very early date, although important branches of the MacLeods were based on the Isles of Harris, Lewis and Raasay. Leod died in 1280 and is buried on Iona; his son Tormod became the first MacLeod (or son of Leod).

The MacDonalds trace their ancestry to Somerled himself. Somerled's second son was called Ranald and Ranald's son Donald became the founder of what would become the main Clan Donald, perhaps the oldest and one of the largest of all the Scottish clans. For many years, the Clan seat was at Duntulm Castle by the start of the Skye Trail in Trotternish, but later moved to Armadale Castle in Sleat. The clan also held the castles of Dunscaith and Knock, also in Sleat.

In 1480 John MacDonald was challenged for the chieftainship of Clan Donald by his bastard son, Angus Og MacDonald. At the Battle of Bloody Bay, William Dubh MacLeod was taken prisoner by Angus Og while supporting John MacDonald but he was severely wounded and died en route to Dunvegan. After the battle, the MacDonalds (now led by Angus Og) raided northern Skye in revenge for MacLeod's part in supporting John. This began years of skirmishes and unrest.

At one stage the MacLeods successfully captured Dunscaith and went on to lay siege to Knock Castle before withdrawing back north. At another battle in Harta Corrie near Glen Sligachan (the entrance is passed on the trail) hundreds were slaughtered and the bodies stacked up around what is now known as the Bloody Stone.

The most notorious of all incidents between the two clans led to the Battle of the Spoiling of the Dyke in 1578. The MacLeods had raided the MacDonald-held Isle of Eigg a couple of years previously, brutally massacring hundreds of MacDonalds by setting fires at the entrance to the cave they had taken refuge in. In revenge the MacDonalds of Uist landed on Skye and barred the doors of Trumpan Church in Waternish when it was full of worshippers. They set it alight, and no-one escaped – except one girl who, though fatally wounded, managed to sound the alarm. The MacLeod chief then set off for Ardmore Bay and almost every MacDonald was killed in the ensuing battle. The corpses were dragged into a turf dyke, giving the battle its name.

Later that century it seemed the rivalry could be mended when Margaret, sister of 15th clan chief Rory Mor MacLeod wed Donald Gorm Mor MacDonald. At that time, it was the custom in the Highlands for a marriage to have a trial period of one year, a tradition known as 'hand-fasting'. If the partnership worked the marriage would become formal, but if not it could be terminated. Margaret bore no children, and according to legend somehow lost an eye (although being one-eyed may have been a euphemism for a number of complaints). When the year was up, legend has it that Donald cast her out on a one-eyed horse, led by a one-eyed servant and accompanied by a one-eyed dog. Not surprisingly, Rory Mor MacLeod was outraged, and a new war began between the clans – The War of the One-Eyed Woman. This culminated in 1601 in a battle in Coire na Creiche (the corrie of the spoils) beneath the Cuillin, when both clans suffered heavy losses. It was the last battle fought between the two clans.

Skye remained a violent place, however. Another tale tells of Hugh MacDonald, a rival to his uncle Chief Donald Gorm, who lived at Caisteal Uisdean, a few miles south of Duntulm. He hatched a plot to kill Donald, but mixed up the letter inviting Donald to Caisteal Uisdean with another which was intended for his hired assassin. Donald therefore got word of the plot and had Hugh imprisoned at Duntulm Castle. He fed him only salt beef through a hole in the roof, and did not allow him any water, until Hugh starved to death, reportedly screaming like a madman as he died.

BONNIE PRINCE CHARLIE AND FLORA MACDONALD

Speed bonnie boat,
like a bird on the wing
Onward the sailors cry
Carry the lad that was born to be king
Over the sea to Skye
Loud the winds howl,
loud the waves roar,
Thunderclaps rend the air
Baffled our foes, stand by the shore
Follow they will not dare.

Nearly 150 years later, a much briefer and less bloody incident was to make the Isle of Skye a household name all over the world, even today, thanks to these lines from 'The Skye Boat Song'.

They tell the story of Bonnie Prince Charlie and Flora MacDonald.

Charles Edward Stuart ('Bonnie Prince Charlie') was the son of James Francis Edward Stuart and grandson of King James II of England (James VII of Scotland), who had been deposed by William of Orange in the Glorious Revolution of 1688. The Jacobite movement was an attempt to restore the Stuarts to the throne. Charles' father James (known as the Old Pretender) headed the first Jacobite rebellion in 1715, but after the inconclusive Battle of Sherrifmuir the rebellion was abandoned for lack of support and James fled back to France. In 1743 James declared his son Charles to be Prince Regent, giving him authority to try to

Bla Bheinn from the head of Glen Sligachan (Stage 5)

recapture the British throne; the stage was set for the 1745 rebellion.

Charles landed in Scotland with just seven companions on the Isle of Eriskay (in the Outer Hebrides) in July. He raised his standard at Glenfinnan on the mainland, and clansmen sympathetic to his cause soon swelled his ranks. Many clan chieftains opted to remain home, including both the Macleod and MacDonald chiefs on Skye, but Charles did manage to raise an army large enough to march on Edinburgh, which he captured conclusively at the Battle of Prestonpans on 21 September. In November he marched southwards into England leading an army of 6000 men. They captured Carlisle and continued to sweep south, reaching as far as Derby. Here, rumours (possibly spread by spies) of a huge government force ahead led Charles and his advisers to decide to turn back. In fact the government army was stranded miles to the north and Charles' continued march into London would have met little resistance.

Back in Scotland and demoralised, many of Charles' men returned to their homes, and the government army, now led by the King's son, the Earl of Cumberland, caught up with the Jacobite forces at Culloden on 16 April 1746. Charles' forces, by now hungry and exhausted, were massacred. Cumberland ordered his men to give no quarter to their opponents, and for the merciless treatment given to wounded and fleeing men, he is

still referred to in the Highlands as Butcher Cumberland.

> Many's the lad fought on that day
> Well the claymore did wield
> When the night came, silently lain
> Dead on Culloden field

Charles himself escaped from the battlefield and his subsequent flight around the Highlands and Islands, pursued by government troops and aided by many Highlanders despite the huge price on his head, has become the stuff of many legends. It was his flight through Skye, however, aided by Flora MacDonald, which is best remembered (see Stage 3 for more details).

> Though the waves heave,
> soft will ye sleep
> Ocean's a royal bed
> Rocked in the deep, Flora will keep
> Watch by your weary head

Charles eventually escaped to France, but the Highlanders did not fare so well in the aftermath of Culloden. Cumberland's army wreaked vengeance across the region. Highland culture was suppressed and the wearing of tartan and even the playing of bagpipes was made a hanging offence. Carrying of arms was outlawed and chiefs were stripped of their traditional powers and slowly became simply landlords. This was the final nail in the coffin of the clan system and the Highland way of life,

Ruins backed by the distant Cuillin ridge (Stage 7)

and paved the way for the Highland Clearances.

> Burned are our homes,
> exile and death
> Scatter the loyal men
> Yet e'er the sword cool in the sheath
> Charlie will come again.

He never did.

THE HIGHLAND CLEARANCES

The period following the catastrophic defeat of the Jacobites at Culloden was a disaster for the Highlands. Cumberland, the leader of the government army, ordered violent reprisals around the region, burning many villages. Of more lasting effect were the laws passed aimed at the subjugation of the Highland clan system. Written

Gaelic was outlawed (even the Bible was not permitted in the language), as was the bearing of arms. Stripped of their powers to raise a fighting force from their men and to attain true independence, the clan chiefs turned their backs on Highland society as they looked for approval from their peers further south; the sponsoring of traditional bards and poets dwindled as the chiefs began to instead to look to impress with lavish southern life-styles. This required money; and there was one obvious way to raise their incomes – through 'improvements' on their estates and the raising of rents. The transformation of the chiefs into landlords had begun.

Initially it was in the chiefs' interest to retain and increase the working population on their land, to help with a booming industry: kelp. This

16

seaweed was used to make soap and other commodities. Many chiefs, such as MacDonald of Sleat, encouraged large families and the subdivision of their lands among their children, so that the farms could no longer support those living on them; instead the people became a source of cheap labour, relocating to the coast to prepare kelp.

The kelp industry collapsed after 1822 when cheaper substitutes became available from Spain, and sheep became the new way for landlords to make money. Skye and the Highlands became vast sheep farms, and the subsistence farmers who had lived there for thousands of years now stood in the way of 'progress'. Many were forced to abandon the best and most fertile land to the sheep, and had to resettle on barren, rocky coastal strips where producing enough food to survive was next to impossible.

Famine became widespread, especially following the potato blights from 1845. For many, voluntary emigration became the only way out; thousands boarded ships to start a new life in America or Canada each year, many dying en route on the crowded boats. Thousands more were forcibly evicted and driven from their torched homes, leaving deserted settlements such as those at Boreraig and Suisnish which are passed on the last day of the Skye Trail. Many Skye folk went to Nova Scotia in Canada where a number of settlements bear Skye placenames, while others headed to Australia, New Zealand and America.

House at Suisnish (Stage 7)

Ruined house at Boreraig (Stage 7)

THE CROFTERS' STRUGGLE

By the end of the 19th century the tide was beginning to turn as crofters began organising themselves to fight back, inspired in part by the land struggle in Ireland. In 1877 the Kilmuir estate in northern Trotternish doubled the rents charged to its crofting tenants. The Factor collected the new rents with some difficulty, with many crofters at first offering partial payment. After he threatened them with eviction – and refused to supply them with seed – they paid in full, but attitudes were beginning to harden. Three years later, tenants on the east side of the estate around Staffin began to withhold the increased portion of their rents. They were led by Norman Stewart, a Valtos crofter and fisherman. Stewart had served a week in prison for taking heather and rushes from the moor to re-thatch his house, something which still rankled. He began agitating for reform and took the nickname 'Parnell' after the Irish Nationalist leader. In 1877 he had refused to pay the rent increase initially but eventually relented. In 1880 there was some confusion over the valuation of his croft, and Stewart again refused to pay in full and was soon joined in this by other crofters. In 1881 the landlord Captain Fraser tried to sway local opinion by sending out packets of tea and sugar to the poorest crofters of Uig, Staffin, Kilmuir and Culnacnoc. Two weeks later he arranged for the Factor to issue eviction warnings on the agitators, especially 'Stewart at Valtos'.

On Easter Monday in Glasgow a public meeting was addressed by the president of the Irish Land League,

Parnell himself. The meeting passed a motion in support of the tenants threatened with eviction in Valtos, pledging to support 'whatever form the struggle might take'. Further public meetings soon passed similar motions; the crofters now had many in Glasgow on their side. As a result Captain Fraser held a meeting with the tenants and both sides accepted a reduction in rents; the crofters had their first taste of what militant action could achieve.

Soon a more serious dispute was breaking out in the Braes south of Portree. A terrible storm on 21 November had sunk 250 Skye fishing boats and increased the general agitation for reduction of rents. A group of young Braes crofters had recently returned from a fishing trip to Kinsale in Ireland where they had learned of the Irish land struggles. Back in the Braes, they persuaded their fellow crofters to sign a petition for the return to common ownership of the grazings on Ben Lee, which had been seized for sheep-farming by Lord MacDonald during the Clearances; until this was granted, they would refuse to pay rents. On 8 December the rents became due, but no Braes crofter arrived at the Factor's office in Portree.

On 7 April 1882 the sheriff's officer Angus Martin headed to the Braes to serve summonses for eviction of the ringleaders. As he approached with his retinue, two boys appeared in the distance and ran off, only to reappear carrying flags, while further boys ran ahead to warn the other crofters. Soon a crowd had gathered, and

Memorial to the Battle of the Braes (Stage 4)

when Martin and his men reached Gedintailor they were surrounded by an angry mob. The summonses were snatched away and burnt in front of Martin, who retreated back to Portree.

The summonses were dropped, but warrants were issued for the arrest of those obstructing Martin and burning the orders. Martin wrote to William Ivory, Sheriff of Inverness, saying that 100 soldiers needed to be stationed in Portree to keep order. On 19 April 40 policemen arrived from Glasgow and together with Sheriff Ivory marched to the Braes.

They arrived at 6am and soon had arrested the five ringleaders. The alarm was raised, however, and 300 Braes folk descended on the police as they took the prisoners back to Portree. They launched a volley of stones, while the Police fought back with truncheons. Women both dealt and received blows, with seven of them being seriously injured by the police. By means of a final charge the police managed to break through and escape with their prisoners. The newspapers dubbed it 'The Battle of the Braes'. The trial of the Braes men was held on 11 May, without jury, and they were found guilty and imprisoned. Soon, however, sympathy for the men grew in the cities; newspapers were outraged and several MPs in the House of Commons demanded an inquiry.

Unrest spread almost immediately to Glendale in the northwest of Skye. The crofters there, led by John MacPherson, were demanding the return of the common grazings of Waterstein. By May several

Boats on Portree Bay (Stage 4)

crofters began grazing their cattle on the land, and court orders issued for their removal were ignored. In November one of the estate shepherds tried to remove the cattle, but he was assaulted by their owners. By Christmas warrants were issued for the arrest of 20 Glendale men involved in the assault, and on 16 January 1883 four policemen were dispatched to new stations around the area. A large crowd had assembled to meet them, and the police were beaten and driven back to Portree. By 20 January even the regular constables stationed at Dunvegan had fled their posts.

Incredibly, an official government emissary was then sent to Skye – aboard a navy gunboat – to negotiate with the Glendale men. It was agreed by the government that a Royal Commission would be set up to investigate the crofters' grievances, and in return a token five crofters agreed to stand trial. They became known as the Glendale martyrs, MacPherson among them, and are commemorated by a memorial in the village today.

On 8 May 1883 Lord Napier began taking evidence from crofters around Skye and the Highlands, and his commission recommended mild reforms. Meanwhile, the Highland Land League (slogan: 'the People are mightier than a Lord') was growing in membership and attracting support from fledgling socialist groups across Scotland; by now there were rent strikes across the Highlands and Islands. In 1885 the League announced its intention to stand candidates for parliament in every Highland and Islands constituency; they won four seats, becoming the first working-class MPs.

Prime Minister William Gladstone relented to pressure and passed the Crofters Act in 1886. This was much more radical than the Napier recommendations, and at last gave every crofter security of tenure. Not only would they be immune from eviction, but they would be able to hand their croft to their heirs.

SKYE TODAY

In the 20th century industrialisation and the Second World War led to more and more people leaving the island. Young men often chose to work abroad for periods of time returning to the homeland in between. Jobs in the central belt of Scotland and south of the border also drew a lot of people who were no longer able to make a decent living from the land. From a population peak of around 23,000 in the 1840s the numbers living on Skye shrank to about 7500 by the late 1960s.

More recently Skye has been bouncing back, powered largely by a thriving tourism industry as well as other opportunities arising partly from the construction of the bridge to the mainland and improvements in modern communication. The last four decades have seen net migration into the island, with Skye a popular destination for active retirees from

England, those wanting to set up tourism businesses, and families with Skye roots seeking a good environment to bring up children. The current population stands at just over 10,000. Today Skye is a mix of tradition and modernity: Gaelic is still spoken by a quarter of the population, there is a well-supported traditional music and ceilidh scene and the crofting lifestyle is kept alive by a myriad of second jobs from postmen to B&B owners, council employees and offshore oil workers.

THE CUILLIN PIONEERS

Imagine Wagner's 'Ride of the Valkyries' frozen in stone and hung up like a colossal screen against the sky. It seems as if Nature, when she hurled The Cuillin up into the light of the sun, said, 'Their scarred ravines shall lead up to towering spires of rock – unlike any other rock so they will never look the same for very long, now blue, now grey, now silver…but…always drenched in mystery and terrors…'
HV Morton, In Praise of Scotland

The Cuillin are indisputably the finest mountains in the British Isles, as well as being the most challenging to climb. HV Morton is just one writer among scores to sing their praises; famous walking writer Hamish Brown described them as 'Mecca – the ultimate', while Ben Humble OBE

claimed 'they have no equal in all the world'. The great Gaelic poet Sorley Maclean also celebrated the Cuillin in poetry.

For many centuries these forbidding peaks were regarded as unclimbable. The Reverend Lesingham Smith and local forester Duncan MacIntyre were the first to scramble here, crossing the Druim Hain ridge while returning from Loch Coruisk to Sligachan. MacIntyre subsequently made repeated unsuccessful attempts to climb Sgurr nan Gillean.

In 1836 Professor James Forbes, an eminent scientist whose exploits in the Alps made him the father of British Mountaineering, hired MacIntyre as guide and together they successfully climbed Sgurr nan Gillean by its southeast ridge. Forbes noted the great steepness of the mountains, but also the roughness of the gabbro rock, writing, 'I have never seen a rock so adapted for clambering.' In 1845 Forbes returned to Skye and, with MacIntyre, made the ascent of Bruach na Frithe, followed by a second ascent of Sgurr nan Gillean, this time by its harder west ridge. Forbes also circumnavigated the range and made the first maps of the Cuillin. Nothing harder was climbed for many years.

In 1857 the poet Algernon Swinburne and Professor John Nicol made the first ascent of Bla Bheinn, probably using the same route commonly in use today from Loch Slapin. In 1865 the Skye man Alexander Nicolson began his years

The Cuillin from the Telford Bridge at Sligachan (Stage 5)

of exploring the range, at the age of 38. He ascended Sgurr nan Gillean, made the first descent of the west ridge by the route now known as Nicolson's Chimney, and continued to Bruach na Frithe.

In 1866 the other great Skye-born climber, John MacKenzie of Sconser, began his Cuillin climbing days by ascending Sgurr nan Gillean at the age of just ten. He was to be a key climber on the Skye scene for the next 50 years. In 1870 he made the first ascent of Sgurr a Ghreadaidh with William Newton Tribe.

In 1873 Alexander Nicolson made the first ascents of Sgurr na Banachdich and Sgurr Dearg. He noted the Inaccessible Pinnacle, writing "It might be possible with ropes and grappling irons to overcome it, but the achievement seems hardly worth the trouble." He then descended and made the first ascent of the highest of the Cuillin peaks via the Great Stone Chute. It is named Sgurr Alasdair (Alexander's Peak) in his honour. In 1874 Nicolson made an epic first ascent of Sgurr Dubh Mor by the Dubhs Ridge (now regarded as Britain's longest rock-climb); he didn't manage to get back to Sligachan until 3am.

In 1880 Willie Naismith, later to be the founder of the Scottish Mountaineering Club, made his first visit to Skye. He climbed the north peak of Bidein Druim nam Ramh. Later in the year Charles and Lawrence Pilkington (of Pilkington Glass fame), two of the greatest climbers of their day, came to the island. They made the first ascent of the Inaccessible Pinnacle, watched

23

by John MacKenzie, who returned to make the second ascent the following year after taking off his shoes. By 1886 Stocker and Parker had ascended the west side of the pinnacle.

In 1887 Charles Pilkington, with MacKenzie, climbed Sgurr Thearlaich, and later Sgurr Mhic Choinnich. The peaks were named in their honour: Sgurr Thearlaich is Gaelic for Charles' peak, while Sgurr Mhic Choinnich is Mackenzie's peak.

By 1888 there was a new name on the crags. Professor John Norman Collie (commonly referred to as Norman Collie) had been inspired to take up mountaineering after watching climbers on Skye a few years earlier. He made many climbs with John MacKenzie (the pair became firm friends and are buried next to each other in Struan cemetery), including a traverse of the ridge from Sgurr a Mhadaidh to Sgurr Thearlaich (using Collie's Ledge on Sgurr Mhic Choinnich). They were finally stopped by the Thearlaich-Dubh gap; afterwards they traversed Sgurr Alasdair and over Bealach Coir'an Lochain before descending to Coruisk, crossing the Druim Hain to Harta Corrie and arriving back at Sligachan at midnight.

By now the main Cuillin summits had been reached, although rock-climbers continue to find new and harder routes right up to the present day. In 1911 Shadbolt and MacLaren made the first complete traverse of the Cuillin Ridge, now regarded as the classic day in British Mountaineering.

It wasn't until 1965 that Hamish MacInnes, Tom Patey, Dave Crabb and Graham Robertson completed the first winter traverse, taking two days. In 1999 top fell-runner Rob Woodall completed an incredible circuit, taking in the Sligachan Red Hills, Garbh-bheinn, the Clach Glas–Bla Bheinn traverse, and the Cuillin Ridge, in just under 24hrs. More recently, Finlay Wild broke his own record for the traverse of the main Cuillin ridge, coming in at just under 3hrs.

While some of the Cuillin pioneers are commemorated in the names of the peaks, climbs and features of the rock themselves, there are plans to erect a sculpture to Collie and MacKenzie at Sligachan in the shadow of the mountains.

GEOLOGY

Skye is a geologist's paradise and is a popular destination for Gore-tex-clad, hammer-wielding academics on field trips. However, the rocks and the scenery formed by them are equally fascinating to non-specialists, and walkers travelling through the landscape on the Skye Trail will get a unique feel for the geology.

Trotternish is dominated by spectacular landslides caused by basaltic lava falling away from the weaker sediments underneath, producing a unique landscape. The whole of the Trotternish ridge is cut away on its eastern side by the largest landslip in Europe, with the dramatic Quiraing and the Old Man of Storr forming the best known features. Where the landslip is still slowly moving into the sea fossils can be found – 170 million year old footprints of the Hadrosaur dinosaur have been found on the beach at Staffin, and Flodigarry and Bearreraig Bay are both popular fossil hunting spots. More fossils and information about local finds are displayed in the excellent Staffin museum situated on the A855 at Ellishadder.

Further on, the trail runs through the shadow of the dramatic Black Cuillin and the Red Hills. The Cuillin – the most majestic mountains in the UK – formed during an intense period of volcanic activity at the time when northwest Europe was splitting from North America and the North Atlantic was formed. The Black Cuillin is mainly made up of gabbro and peridotite and the Red Hills from red-coloured granite. These rocks were formed about 55 million years ago, just the blink of an eye in geological terms. The ice and frost of the Ice Age (between 26,000 and 13,000 years ago) took its toll on this landscape, forming dramatic corries, arêtes and the superb glacial trough and basin in which Loch Coruisk sits. Frost has shattered rocks from the cliffs and pinnacles of the Cuillin, forming many scree slopes. The melting of the glaciers at the end of the ice age caused the land to slowly rise once the weight of the ice was removed.

Landslipped ground below Bioda Buidhe (Stage 2)

This produced the many classic raised beaches which can be seen around the coast of Skye, including at Staffin where the road to the slipway has been built on this landform.

At its southern end Skye has some of the oldest rocks in world. These rocks – in Sleat and southeastern Skye – are more than 450 million years old and include Lewisian gneiss, Torridonian sandstone, shales, schists, quartzites and limestones.

WILDLIFE AND PLANTS

Skye has an abundance of interesting plants and wildlife and exploring on foot increases your chance of an exciting encounter. Its well worth taking a lightweight pair of binoculars and keeping them accessible while walking.

Due to the combination of the wide variety of habitats (upland moorland, croftland, lochside, woodland, sea-shore) and the relatively mild climate of the island, the route taken by the Skye Trail takes in a huge diversity of plantlife. Crossing the peaty land to reach Rubha Hunish at the very start of the trek in summer you are likely to encounter yellow bog aphosdel, emerging from the grass like golden sparklers. These are also known as bone breakers as they were once thought to be responsible for broken legs in cows. Today we understand that aphosdel thrives in areas of low calcium and it is this lack of mineral in the cows' diet which led to their weak bones. It is also worth looking out for orchids in this area – Skye is home to at least 17 different varieties.

Razorbill at Rubha Hunish (Stage 1)

The Trotternish ridge is designated as a Special Conservation Area because of its rare plantlife, which includes alpines such as the very rare Iceland Purslane. Unless you are extremely eagle-eyed, however, you are more likely to encounter tormentil, field gentian, wild thyme, both ling and bell heather, mountain crowberry, saxifrages, and roseroot (locally called the Trotternish Rose), which is often found growing from inaccessible rock ledges.

Looking to the skies, the trail offers a great chance to see some of the UK's most spectacular birds, including golden and white-tailed eagles, peregrine falcons and seabirds such as great skuas and gannets visiting on fishing trips.

Eagles

The magnificent white-tailed (or sea) eagle is Britain's largest and rarest bird of prey. Once spotted they are fairly easy to distinguish, with a brown body, pale head and neck, and white tail feathers. Sea eagles have a slightly scruffy look and when in flight their massive wings have clear-fingered ends and a wedge-shaped tail. The bird was persecuted to the point of extinction by 1930 and the current population of around 16 breeding pairs on Skye is thanks to a reintroduction project begun on the Isle of Rum the 1970s. There is now a healthy population along much of the west Scottish coast and a more recent reintroduction project is currently underway in southeast Scotland.

The Aros Centre just outside Portree, and passed on the Skye Trail, has a year-round sea eagle exhibition with live footage (April–October) from a nearby nest. If you do spot a sea eagle, identification can often be confirmed by the large coloured tags on the wings – the letter/number combination on the tag will be useful to the sea eagle project if you report a sighting to the RSPB. White-tailed eagles are less shy of humans than golden eagles and can frequently be seen in pairs during the breeding season. They often feed on carrion and if you are lucky enough to spot one after a good feed it may well hang around the same spot for a lengthy period while it digests its meal. As well as carrion, sea eagles eat a lot of fish, and also rabbits, hares and birds, particularly fulmars. They will also steal prey caught by other birds and even otters.

The breeding sites are kept secret due to the threat from egg hunters and others. Sea eagles breed for the first time when they are 5 or 6 years old. The adult birds form life-long bonds with their mate, although they will seek a new mate if one of the pair dies. They live for an average of 21 years, with the oldest recorded bird being 30 years old. Sometimes you can hear the male's loud and frequent calling during the breeding season. Sea eagles put on an aerial courtship display which can involve the pair locking claws mid-air and undertaking a series of tumbling cart-wheels before soaring upwards at the last minute. Both the male and female take part in building a large nest that they may use for many years. Eggs are laid in March and April with a six-week incubation period in which the female does most of the sitting on the eggs. The male provides all the food for the first three weeks after the chicks hatch and then the male and female take turns to leave the nest to hunt. The chicks leave the nest at about ten weeks old, although they remain nearby and dependent on their parents for another six weeks.

Otters

You are more likely to see otters swimming off the coastline rather than on land. In the water otters can often be identified by the V-shaped wake just behind them as they swim with only the front of their head visible. Expert swimmers, they dive for food, their favourite being fish, such as butterfish, from the seabed. They also eat birds, small mammals, frogs and crabs. Otters have an acute sense of smell, sight and hearing and will often disappear if they become aware of your presence. On land you can look for the distinctive otter spraint marks. These are otter droppings – usually white from the high fish bone content, and forming small fertile mounds of bright green grass. These sites are used to mark territory and provide a form of communication to other otters through smell. You can often trace the

regular routes taken by an otter by following from one spraint marking to the next.

You are most likely to see an otter on land at dawn or dusk and you may well see one while driving around the island, but take care as they have very little road sense and traffic accidents are a big threat to the otter population here.

Otters tend to live alone, although cubs will stay with their mother for between 11 and 15 months. They are often larger than people expect, with an adult being between 1 and 1.3m in length and weighing 7 to 9kg. Sometimes you may see something in the water and dismiss it as a seal, but it is often worth having a look with binoculars in case it is an otter.

Seals

Seals, both common and grey (or harbour), can often be seen around the coastline of Skye – on a wet walk their curiosity is guaranteed to raise the spirits. Seals will often watch you from the water, lazily bobbing like floating bottles, before diving for up to 10 minutes at a time.

Common seals vary in colour from brownish black to tan or grey. The body and flippers are short, with a proportionately large, rounded head. The nostrils appear distinctively V-shaped. They may reach an adult length of 1.85m and a weight of 130kg; females are generally smaller. Female common seals have a lifespan of 30–35 years while male lifespans

Grey seals at Flodigarry (Stage 1)

are usually 20–25. Scientists have suggested that this is due to the stresses male seals are subjected to during breeding seasons. Although preferring to live in colonies, seals are defensive of their own space and can often be seen defending their own area of rock by flapping apparently ineffectively with a flipper at any intruder and making a distinctive 'blowing a raspberry' noise. If approached by humans seals will often head straight into the water where they are more mobile and safer.

The grey seal is the largest native mammal in Britain, with the bulls reaching an enormous 2.5–3.3m long and weighing up to 300kg; the cows are much smaller, typically 1.6–2m long and 100–150kg in weight. During the winter months they can be seen hauled out on the rocks, islands and shoals not far from shore.

Like common seals, the grey seal eats mainly fish and crustaceans.

CULTURE, MUSIC AND LANGUAGE

Skye has a strong musical tradition reaching back through the centuries, and for an island of only 10,000 people it has given the world a long list of renowned artists in a surprising variety of genres.

The island has had a particularly strong tradition of piping dating back to the mid 16th century. Duirinish was home to the MacCrimmon family, hereditary pipers to the MacLeods. The long laments (known as Pibrochs) such as the 'Lament for the Children' by Padraig Mor MacCrimmon and the 'Lament for Mary Macleod' by his son Padraig Og

The Isle of Skye Pipe Band in action

MacCrimmon are thought by many to be among the greatest glories of Scottish, let alone Gaelic, culture.

Songs have also been prominent through the centuries, with the late-19th-century Màiri Mhòr nan Òran (Great Mary of the Songs) being particularly prominent. Her radical songs celebrated the islanders' struggle against oppression.

Far from declining, the island's musicians have if anything become even more prominent in recent times. Most famous of the more modern Skye bands is Runrig, the Celtic rock band, many of whose songs have Gaelic lyrics. Runrig gained a huge following through the 1980s and 1990s and although lead singer Donnie Munro left the group and began a solo career (as well as a

spell as a politician), the group do still perform occasionally at concerts. Other popular Skye bands on the folk circuit include the well-known Peat Bog Faeries, whose music combines traditional instruments with driving up-tempo beats, and Cliar, the 'Gaelic supergroup' featuring close vocal harmonies, pipes and harp. DJ and dance musician Mylo (otherwise known as Myles MacInnes) hails from Sleat at the southern end of the island, and there is a wealth of local bands and performers with local ceilidhs a great way to experience this.

The Aros Centre at Portree has concerts featuring many top artists, and there are regular ceilidhs and dances held all around the island – to find one look in the local weekly newspaper, the West Highland Free Press.

A heavyweight athlete, or 'heavy', prepares to throw the hammer at the Isle of Skye Highland Games

Skye remains an outpost of spoken Gaelic, with Trotternish in the north of the island a particular stronghold. More recently the growth of the Gaelic college, Sabal Mòr Ostaig, in Sleat has seen a resurgence of interest in Gaelic and Gaelic-medium teaching in schools in the southern part of the island. Sabhal Mòr Ostaig hosts a number of short courses as well as well as providing degree-level education in Gaelic. Some primary schools now teach wholly in Gaelic, although most split the teaching with English as the High School in Portree does. Most road signs will have both the Gaelic and English placenames and usually they are easy to translate, for example Portree becomes Port Righ, meaning Kings Port.

Religion has long been an important part of island life, and although church attendance is falling, even many small settlements have a choice of churches. The Church of Scotland and the Free Church are the most popular and many people still observe the Sabbath, so in smaller settlements don't rely on shops or cafés being open on Sundays.

Attending a shinty match is usually a memorable experience of rough and tumble as the rules allow the curved stick, or caman, to be used for tackling as well as trying to get the ball into the goal. Games are played in Portree on Saturdays during the season (March–October) and these and other Skye fixtures are noted in the local paper, the *West Highland Free Press*.

PREPARATION AND PLANNING

The Skye Trail is a tough, uncompromising route requiring self-reliance, good equipment, navigation skills and previous experience of hillwalking and backpacking. If you have previously completed other Scottish long-distance routes such as the West Highland Way or the Great Glen Way then do not expect similar facilities or terrain. This is an un-waymarked trail – often on pathless ground – passing through some fairly remote areas, and the weather is notoriously unpredictable. However, good preparation can make these challenges part of the attraction, allowing you to reach parts of the island very few people visit, and providing a profound sense of achievement.

WHEN TO GO

Unpredictability is the one thing you can be sure of when it comes to Skye weather. However, generally speaking the spring and summer are likely to be the best months for walking on Skye, with early May being popular to avoid the midges. The long daylight hours from June to the end of August make it possible to cover large distances. Accommodation can get booked up in July and August and peak weekends throughout the year.

Although not impossible, undertaking the Skye Trail in winter is likely to be extremely challenging given the very short daylight hours, closure of some accommodation and facilities and the probability of winter storms. The wind – with frequent storms – in

The Skye Bridge

particular can become a major problem as well as the possibility of snow and ice on the hills.

TRAVEL

If travelling to the UK from outside the EU you may need a visa which can sometimes take time to arrange so its worth checking this at the early planning stages. Glasgow and Edinburgh airports have a wide range of regular international flights and Inverness is also worth considering as a destination, with plenty of domestic flights and some flights from the EU including a budget airline link from Amsterdam.

Citylink buses ply their way direct to Portree from both Glasgow and Inverness. These are an excellent option for those attempting the Skye Trail as you can take the Citylink bus to Portree (www.citylink.co.uk) and then use the local bus which loops around the Trotternish peninsula to reach Duntulm at start of the trail. The Citylink bus can then be picked up from the end of the trail in Broadford for the return trip.

While the opening of the Skye Bridge in 1995 (now toll free) has made it much easier to get to Skye, many still prefer the romance of arriving 'over the sea to Skye' and both the year-round Mallaig ferry to Armadale and the Skye Ferry which runs during the summer months between Glenelg and Kylerhea make this an enjoyable option. If driving all the way, allow 5–6hrs from Glasgow, or 2½hrs from Inverness. Both are fantastic routes covering some spectacular Highland scenery.

If you have a non-walking companion willing to act as a driver, every stage of the trail finishes at a road so it is perfectly possible to do the route from the same or a number of accommodation bases. All the roads crossed on the route are served by local buses, some with more regular services than others – check timetables with Stagecoach Highlands (www.stagecoachbus.com). It is also possible to make use of a taxi to get to accommodation – it is easier and cheaper to arrange this in advance rather than relying on being able to phone on the day. It should be noted that mobile reception is weak or non-existent in many places on the island and cannot be relied on. On Skye itself hitching is still a frequently used means of getting about, although the usual precautions should be taken and there is no guarantee you will be picked up especially if you have a hefty backpack of wet kit.

MONEY AND COMMUNICATIONS

There are banks (with 24-hour ATMs) in Portree and Broadford and post offices in Staffin, Portree, Elgol and Broadford. Many B&Bs, campsites and cafés do not take card payments so it is useful to have a good supply of cash. Mobile phone reception is patchy and should not be relied on

Sligachan campsite (Stage 4)

to book accommodation or taxis. Accommodation providers on the island increasingly offer WiFi, but connections can be slow and there are some areas without broadband at all so its best to check before booking if getting online is important to you.

ACCOMMODATION

As one of Scotland's most popular tourist destinations, the Isle of Skye is bursting with accommodation options – however, in the peak summer months that accommodation can be full to capacity and therefore booking ahead is advisable. It should also be noted that some hostels and B&Bs close for the winter when the island is considerably less busy. The Skye Trail has been designed so that there

is access to accommodation from the end of every stage, but it also makes a great backpacking route, with official campsites at Portree, Sligachan and Flodigarry, and innumerable wild camping options for the experienced backpacker.

Bed & Breakfasts are also a good option; with rooms and breakfast provided in the owner's house its a good way to meet locals and get a real feel for modern-day life on the island. Not all B&Bs serve evening meals and you may have to ask in advance if you want a packed lunch for the next day. Hotels provide the opportunity to mix with other travellers and provide an evening meal. Within the B&B and hotel sector there is accommodation to suit a wide range of budgets, although you may find steep single supplements are imposed in the high summer. There are hostels at Flodigarry, Portree, Sligachan and Broadford and these, too, often need to be booked in advance.

It is also possible to do the route while staying at a holiday cottage or a couple of hotels/B&Bs, as long as you have a willing driver to deposit and pick you up for each day's stage. This provides the advantage of not having to carry much gear and enjoying the home comforts of a single base, but many long-distance walkers relish the variety and excitement of staying in a different place every night as the journey progresses.

A number of companies are now also offering Skye Trail packages, either as self-guided walk, with baggage carried for you and accommodation booked, or as a guided walk as part of a group holiday (see Appendix C). The Highland Council Ranger Service has also divided the route up into a number of day walks and have offered these as one-off, single-day guided walks in the past – check out the Highland Council website for details (www.highland.gov.uk). See Appendix B for a selection of accommodation options available along the route at the time of going to press.

WHAT TO TAKE

A lot will depend on whether you are backpacking the route and need to carry camping equipment, but in general your enjoyment of the route will be enhanced by getting the balance

Setting off on the coast path to Boreraig (Stage 7)

right between carrying as lightweight a pack as possible while still having enough gear to be safe and comfortable. Using a baggage transfer service to move your bags between accommodation is also an option.

Gear will usually include rucksack, waterproofs (jacket and overtrousers), layering system of clothes including wickable base layer, hat and gloves and sunhat (if you are an optimist), walking boots, water bottle, torch, whistle, first aid kit, compass and map, survival bag or emergency shelter, rucksack liner or dry bags. Optional extras include mobile phone/GPS, midge repellent (essential if camping in summer), walking poles, camera, binoculars, sunglasses, suntan lotion.

Additional gear for the backpacker should include tent, sleeping mat, sleeping bag, stove, fuel (re-supply possible in Portree), pans, cutlery, knife, water sterilisation tablets, and don't forget the matches or lighter.

NAVIGATION AND MAPS

Harvey Maps have produced a single map for the Skye Trail on waterproof paper. Harvey mapping is slightly different to Ordnance Survey mapping, but many walkers prefer it once accustomed to its unique look. The trail is also covered by 1:25,000 OS Explorer maps 408 (Trotternish), 410 (Portree), 411 (Cuillin Hills) and 412 (Sleat), or by two 1:50,000 Landranger maps, 23 (North Skye) and 32 (South Skye). It is also possible to print out the relevant mapping sections from digital mapping programmes or from the Skye Trail website www.skyetrail.org.uk

Red Hills from the marble line (Stage 7)

(1:25,000 OS maps available if you register); however, the hazard of these loose sheets getting wet and the ink running, or being blown away, and the fact that they may not cover enough ground to show escape routes or detours, mean that carrying a proper map as well is prudent. Given the island's reputation for rain, keeping maps in a waterproof case is recommended.

A dedicated GPS or smartphone with mapping is a great addition to carrying a paper map and compass. You can follow a GPS route downloaded from the Skye Trail website or use the device to quickly locate your position, and many people successfully use them regularly as their main means of navigating. However, you still need to be able to read and interpret a map. Spare batteries should be carried and electronic gadgets should not be wholly relied upon as they may break or run out of charge.

The glossary in Appendix D may help you learn to recognise some of the Gaelic terms used on the maps as you go along.

While this guidebook aims to be as up-to-date as possible, any changes in the route can be checked at the Skye Trail website, where any access problems can also be reported.

ACCESS

The Land Reform (Scotland) Act 2003 gave walkers the right of access over most Scottish land away from residential buildings. These generous rights come with a set of responsibilities on the part of the walker, which include respecting other users of the land and minimising the environmental impact and disturbance to wildlife. Skye is still a predominantly crofting area which means plenty of open grazing land with many sheep and some cattle, often unfenced even in clifftop situations. In these areas **dogs** can cause serious problems and there has been at least one case of a sheep being chased over a cliff by an uncontrolled dog. Always follow the Scottish Outdoor Access Code, keeping dogs under tight control during spring and early summer and in livestock grazing areas to avoid disturbing animals and also any ground-nesting birds.

The rights and responsibilities of **wild campers** are also set out in the Access Code. You are allowed to wild camp with lightweight equipment, in small groups, for only two or three nights in one place, wherever access rights apply but not in enclosed fields of crops or animals, and you must keep well away from buildings, roads or historic structures. You should pack out all litter, remove all traces of your pitch and take care not to cause pollution when going to the toilet or washing pots and pans.

Deer stalking is not normally an issue for walkers on the Isle of Skye. Compared to Scottish mainland estates, red deer numbers are small and there is no commercial stalking on estates covering the Skye Trail.

However, walkers should be aware that deer management involving the culling of animals may be taking place and should avoid disturbing any shoots if stalkers are seen near the route.

The official code for responsible behaviour – including a guide to wild camping – is available on the www.outdooraccess-scotland.co.uk website.

WEATHER

But if you are a delicate man,
And of wetting your skin you are shy,
I'd have you know, before you go,
You had better not think of Skye!
from Alexander Nicolson's
The Isle of Skye, 1862

Sited on the far west of Britain, the Isle of Skye benefits from the warming effects of the gulf stream and has a generally mild climate for somewhere this northerly. However, no land mass protects it from the Atlantic Ocean and it is therefore subject to strong winds and higher-than-average rainfall. For the walker this means being prepared for most weather conditions – it is often said that on Skye you may face all four seasons in one day.

The north of the island is more exposed to the wind (note the general lack of trees on the Trotternish peninsula) but also has less rain than central and southern Skye. Winds in excess of 80 miles an hour have been recorded, something to bear in mind

Beinn Edra in winter (Stage 2)

when tackling the exposed section of the Trotternish Ridge, particularly if you are planning on wild camping; the ridge is frequently battered by gales in the autumn and winter. May is the sunniest and driest month, with less rainfall on average from March to June. However, the main point to remember about the climate on Skye is that it is unpredictable and that changeable conditions can bring out the best in the amazing scenery. Having said that, its always useful to check whether there are drying facilities where you intend to stay.

MIDGES AND TICKS

The peak season for midges is from mid to late May to early October and how seriously they affect you will be down to the weather, the number of midges around that year, whether you are camping and just how tasty you are to the 'wee beasties'.

The tiny black Scottish midge, *Culicoides Impuctatus*, bites exposed flesh, usually causing only a mild reaction – it's the constant buzzing and landing on your skin that is often the biggest irritant – although the bites can swell and be very itchy on a minority of people. Generally midges are only a serious problem from July to September for campers wanting to cook and lounge around the campsite. Midges prefer damp, overcast and windless days and are most active early in the morning and late evening. They cannot fly in even

a fairly light breeze so exposed sections of the route are often midge-free. They also hate strong sunshine and are attracted to pools of water. Walkers are divided over the best midge repellents; anything containing DEET is likely to be the most effective but many people don't like the strong chemicals. Recently some walkers have been recommending Smidge – a newcomer to the market developed by those behind the midge forecast, a daily prediction of likely midge levels (www.midgeforecast. co.uk). If camping in the peak season then a mesh midge hood can be a wise investment.

Ticks are not a huge problem on the island but you should still keep an eye out for these creatures that latch on to unsuspecting walkers to feed on their blood. The bites often go unnoticed so you should check yourself at the end of each day for these poppy-seed sized creatures and carefully remove any that you find. There is a danger (slight on Skye where infected ticks are still rare) of contracting the debilitating Lyme Disease so watch any bite sites for a characteristic bulls-eye red swelling and cold-like symptoms, and seek medical advice if you're worried. Many insect repellents are also effective against ticks and taking precautions like wearing loose long-sleeved clothing and tucking trousers into socks will also help.

SAFETY AND EMERGENCIES

Sudden weather changes are a way of life on Skye and you need to plan accordingly and be equipped for rain as well as excessive heat and cold conditions. Heavy rainfall or snowmelt can make burns (streams) impassable – the place where this is most likely to be a problem is the final approach to Sligachan on Stage 4 – if in doubt turn back; there are also burn crossings on the next stage along Glen Sligachan which can become impassable in spate conditions. If tackling the alternative Stage 5 over Bla Bheinn be especially aware of the weather conditions. Both this peak and the Trotternish Ridge would require mountaineering equipment for snow and ice in winter.

While this part of Scotland is blessed with long hours of daylight in the summer months, the route crosses a lot of rough, pathless terrain that may take longer than anticipated. Plenty of time should be allowed to complete each section comfortably in daylight – this applies in particular to the long second stage, from Flodigarry to the Storr.

Some sections of the route (particularly along the Trotternish Ridge and down Glen Sligachan to Camasunary) are remote and a long way from road or any help. It is good practice to think about possible escape routes on these sections before setting out. If camping out on the Trotternish Ridge it should be noted that there are few quick ways off the ridge, the route is

Descending from Bla Bheinn (Stage 6B)

Sgurr nan Gillean seen from Glen Sligachan (Stage 5)

very exposed and can be difficult to navigate in poor visibility.

If you do get into trouble and need help call 999 or 112 and ask for the Police and then Mountain Rescue. Before you call try to get as much information as possible about your location, preferably an accurate grid reference, and the condition of any casualties. Skye's Mountain Rescue Team has an excellent reputation and many of the volunteers who make up its numbers work as mountain guides or are enthusiastic walkers and climbers themselves. However, they are all volunteers and a rescue call out should always be the last resort. If you have left details of your route with others, remember to let them know when you have finished.

USING THIS GUIDE

An overview of the seven stages (and one alternative stage) described in this book is included in Appendix A, to help with planning your route. Each section of the route is accompanied by an extract from the Ordnance Survey 1:50,000 map. An information box gives the start and finish point, distance (km/miles) and total ascent (to the nearest 5m), the approximate time taken to complete the stage, the terrain that will be encountered, and the map (or maps) needed. Within the route description text, points of interest are included to help you make the most of your visits to places along the way. It is important to remember that times quoted for each stage are approximations only, and make no

Sunset over Broadford (Stage 7)

allowance for rest stops, picnics, or interruptions to take photographs.

The times are based on our experience on a number of different outings in various weather conditions for each section of the route, taking into account that most people will be carrying a multi-day pack. However, we walk at a slower pace than many and the times probably err on the generous side. The distances and ascent figures were recorded on the ground by GPS and the GPS waypoints can be downloaded from the Walkhighlands website (www.walkhighlands.co.uk).

You can also get a feel for how other people have experienced the route by reading other walkers' trip reports on the Skye Trail website (www.skyetrail.org.uk).

Route profiles have been provided (where helpful) to give a rough idea of the undulating nature of the route in a simplified form. They do not attempt to give an accurate representation of every up and down experienced along the way.

Boxes in the text describe in more detail in features of interest seen along the way.

THE SKYE TRAIL

View down the path to Rubha Hunish (Stage 1)

STAGE 1
Rubha Hunish to Flodigarry

Start	Shulista turn off from A855 at red phone box, Kilmaluag (NG 422 742)
Finish	Flodigarry Hostel (NG 464 719)
Distance	11.5km (7½ miles) (excludes detour out to the point)
Total Ascent	290m
Time	5½–6½hrs (plus 1½hrs to explore the Rubha Hunish Headland)
Terrain	Rough going, boggy and pathless for much of the way. Optional easy scramble down to the headland. Livestock grazing on croftland so dogs should be kept under tight control
Maps	Harvey – The Skye Trail; OS Explorer 408 Trotternish; OS Landranger 23 North Skye

Rubha Hunish is one of the most magical spots on Skye – a scenically spectacular haven for seabirds and marine mammals. Every visit to this most northerly tip of the island rewards with different sights, sounds and windy blasts. The hardy can wild camp right out on the headland or use the tiny old coastguard lookout turned walkers' bothy, but others may prefer to start after catching the morning bus from Portree which loops around the Trotternish peninsula (the Duntulm Hotel and B&Bs are also nearby). Either way make sure you leave plenty of time to enjoy this special place before beginning the long walk south in earnest.

After the visit out to the headland, the majority of the walk follows the clifftops of the dramatic coastline, crossing croftland where sheep will be your main companions. The stage ends at Flodigarry, once home to Flora MacDonald, and now boasting a walker-friendly hostel and plush hotel. The nearest B&Bs are in the strung-out township of Staffin – a pick-up could be arranged – where there are also a couple of cafés, two shops and a campsite.

WHALE-WATCHING AT RUBHA HUNISH

During July and August the sea just off the furthest point of Rubha Hunish is a popular feeding place for minke whales. Probably the best location in the UK for watching these massive mammals from the coastline, it is not a rare experience to be able to sit here and watch one circling for quite some time. The point is also visited by porpoises and dolphins, which tend to be more purposeful and pass by relatively quickly.

Minke whales grow up to 10m in length and the best time of year to see them is from mid June to the end of September. On a day when the sea is relatively calm you can focus on any surface disturbance, and dull skies reduce the amount of glare reflected from the water. The whales will often hang around the same feeding spot for half a day or more. Scan the sea backwards and forwards with binoculars looking for any signs of disturbance and remember that once you have spotted a whale it is likely to come up to breathe three to five times before heading down for a much longer dive, after which it can be difficult to gauge where it will pop up again. Their dives are interspersed with a small puff from their blow hole, which is useful for alerting you to the first sighting or watching their progress if they are on the move.

Often solitary, minke whales can sometimes be spotted in small groups. They are grey and sleek and tend not to breach the water completely – this means that by the time you press the camera button they are often already back underwater and your photo shows nothing more than a disturbed bit of sea! Feeding seabirds can sometimes alert you to the presence of whales and other marine mammals feeding on the same shoal.

As well as minke whales, the waters around the west coast of Scotland are an important habitat for dolphins and porpoises. Twenty-four different species of sea mammal have been spotted in these waters, from the huge and very rare blue whale to the small and more common harbour porpoise. The smallest cetacean in British waters, the harbour porpoise can often be seen in groups, sometimes surfing in breaking waves.

There is something incredibly satisfying about looking out to sea from a high headland at the furthest tip of an island, and **Rubha Hunish** provides the perfect starting point for the long walk south. Rubha Hunish has spectacular columnar basalt cliffs, a superb view out over the Minch towards the Outer Hebrides and remarkable wildlife.

The walk begins from the small car park just east of the telephone box which marks the junction of the Shulista road with the A855 which winds its way around the Trotternish peninsula.

From the car park near the phone box walk over the cattle grid and turn immediately left onto a clear path. This follows a low escarpment as it heads north northwest across moorland. Soon the remains of the settlement of Erisco can be seen at the rear of **Duntulm Bay**. The row of ruined cottages and byres that made up the crofting township has been deserted since 1765.

When a kissing gate in a fence is reached follow the path uphill northwards onto **Meall Tuath**. A small flat-roofed building becomes visible ahead – continue uphill here following a raised dyke. About halfway up bear off to the left along a small path and then climb directly up to the hut.

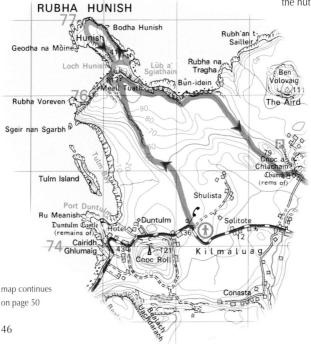

map continues
on page 50

This is a former **coastguard lookout** overlooking the Little Minch, an important shipping channel. The hut was once manned around the clock, and offers excellent shelter on a wild day. Today it is maintained by volunteers from the Mountain Bothy Association as a shelter for walkers and is a wonderful place to escape the elements while scanning the seas for passing whales, porpoises and even the odd massive oil rig being towed through the Minch.

Duntulm Castle from the path

The location is spectacular, with great vertical cliffs just to the north plunging down 100m and magnificent views across the sea to the mountains on the Isle of Harris, with Toddun the most prominent.

Detour to the Hunish

From the lookout, follow the path along the cliff edge to the left (west southwest) near the fence. The path soon descends into a hollow beneath two higher sections of cliff. Go over the stile and then over the second stile before bearing right to go through a kissing gate next to a giant boulder which sits close to the cliff edge. On the far side of this boulder the steep descent to the **Hunish** headland begins. The descent down to the ancient raised beach far below is much less difficult than it looks, following a series of natural rocky steps with some protection from the exposure, although care should be taken especially in wet weather or with a heavy pack. Scramble down the trickier section to join the clearer grassy path seen below. Great columns of basalt – similar to those on Staffa and at the Giant's Causeway in Northern Ireland – soar above.

Once down on the relatively flat ground head over to the right (east) side of the headland where there is a deep geo, or rocky inlet, and a bay where gannets can often be seen diving for food having flown from their breeding ground on faraway St Kilda. Work your way around the far side of the headland taking care near the cliff edge.

There are a couple of large sea stacks beside **the Hunish**, and the remains of rope slings are evidence that climbers have conquered these dolerite columns. During nesting season the air is often alive with whirling birds, kittiwakes, razorbills and shags. Great skuas sometimes soar menacingly overhead, and puffins can sometimes be seen out on the water during the summer months. At the northern tip of the Hunish the waters from either side of the headland clash in a sea of turbulence. It is here that you stand the best chance of spotting whales.

Keep following the headland anti-clockwise to eventually start heading back towards the cliff high above Loch Hunish.

Loch Hunish provides the best opportunity to spot **otters**. Look for the distinctive V-shape they make in the water. Otters need regular access to fresh water to clean their coats and you may be able to spot their runs through the grass to the pools in the centre of the peninsula. The bright green topped grassy mounds are also signs of an active otter colony. If you examine these humps carefully the fish bones and other debris known as otter spraint can be seen; it is this nitrogen-rich waste that feeds the lush grass growth and marks the territory of the male dog otters.

Return up the rocky path which would have originally been used by crofters from Erisco who grew crops down on the Hunish.

If you glance back down you may be able to make out the ridges and furrows of the **lazy bed system** where seaweed was piled up between drainage ditches to fertilise the poor soil to grow barley, oats or potatoes. Examples of the heavy implements used can be seen at the nearby Museum of Island Life in Kilmuir – proof that there was nothing lazy about this method at all.

Clamber back up the path then bear left (east) at the clifftop to return to the lookout bothy.

Heading east along the clifftops

Now follow the vague path, to the left of a line of metal fence posts, eastwards along the coastline. Near the cliff edge keep to the right of a fence, cross a boggy dip and take the small path cutting across a minor headland aiming towards the small peak, Ben Volovaig, which can be seen on the horizon. Cross a stile at a fence and bear right to aim southeast along slightly higher ground. When a prominent knoll comes into view straight ahead, a muddy vehicle track can be picked up. Before a dip in the ground turn right and go through a gap in an old stone wall and follow the grassy track to reach the ruins of **St Moluag's Church**. Continue to the road and turn right along it.

When the road bends right, go straight ahead through a kissing gate onto a path that leads to a footbridge over a burn. On the far side turn left and continue round the coastline, aiming for a whitewashed crofthouse. Pass to the right of this to reach the road end at **Balmacqueen**.

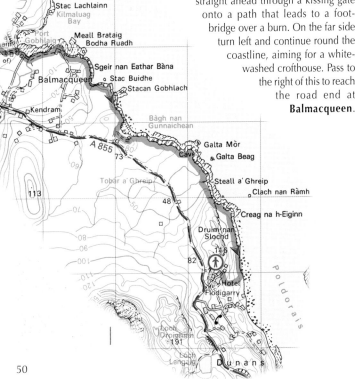

Do not turn up the road. Instead cross over a stile to take to the shore, keeping on the seaward side of the crofting land. Soon the coastline rises to another stile; cross this and continue up by the clifftops – taking care as the unprotected cliff edge is right by the route at a corner. Eventually the walk follows a line of old posts over the undulating ground just back from the coastal cliffs, finally reaching a track coming up from the road where there was a radar station during the Second World War. ▶

As the walk continues along the cliffs, basaltic columns can be seen twisted into strange shapes and some have eroded to stand as lonely sea stacks.

There is no path along the cliffs and the way can be very wet underfoot in places, with a burn to cross which could be difficult in very wet conditions. On the far side carefully cross the fence and follow the fence-line uphill, staying on the landward side to reach a stile. Climb this and then descend a steep grassy rake, taking care to keep away from the cliff edge on your left. Once down to the lower level simply follow the coast to approach the wide sweeping arc of Staffin Bay, with **Eilean Flodigarry** prominent just out to sea. At the seashore look out for a clear path climbing up on the right at the back of the bay which soon passes an interpretative carved slab. Follow the path inland to **Flodigarry**, a tiny, scattered settlement that includes the hotel and hostel.

Shoreline at Flodigarry

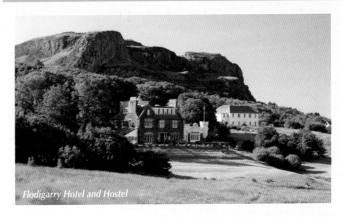

Flodigarry Hotel and Hostel

Dun Flodigarry Hostel is the large square white building up to the right; take the rough path to the right to reach it by crossing the second of the two stiles. The hostel is open all year, and has both dorm beds and private rooms. It sells some basic food and also has a camping area; walkers wild camping elsewhere can pay a nominal charge to use the showers and self-catering facilities.

The Flodigarry Hotel next door provides plusher accommodation and bar meals as well as a slice of history, as one of the buildings was once home to local heroine Flora MacDonald. After famously rowing across the Minch with Bonnie Prince Charlie disguised as her servant, Flora became quite a celebrity in later life, and entertained Johnson and Boswell during their tour of the isles.

Further south along the A855 are the scattered settlements making up the township of Staffin. You may be able to catch the bus or meet a pre-arranged pick-up from one of its numerous B&Bs; Staffin has two shops and cafés, including Columba 1400 which has internet access. There is a campsite right at the furthest end of the village which would add a considerable hike to your day. For wild campers suitable spots can be found a little further along the next stage of the Skye Trail.

Accommodation and Facilities

Dun Flodigarry Hostel www.hostelflodigarry.co.uk 01470 552212

Achtalean B&B (run by enthusiastic hillwalkers, near the Village Stores) www.achtalean.co.uk 01470 562723

Bealach Uige B&B (friendly B&B on the far side of Staffin)
www.skyeaccommodation-staffin.co.uk 01470 562434

Ceol na Mara B&B www.ceolnamara.co.uk 01470 562242

Dunmar B&B www.dunmarbandb.co.uk 01470 562411

Gairloch View B&B (at Digg, Staffin, the nearest B&B to the end of the stage)
www.gairlochview.co.uk 01470 562718

The Flodigarry Hotel (upmarket accommodation, restaurant and bar meals,
adjacent to the Hostel) www.flodigarry.co.uk 01470 552203

Camping – Dun Flodigarry Hostel or Staffin Campsite (on the far side of Staffin)
www.staffincampsite.co.uk 01470 562213

Shops – small Village Stores selling a good range of groceries, and petrol (on
A855 at back of Staffin Bay); also Staffin Stores (further round towards Portree
next to the Oystercatcher Café) sells a wide range of food, including hot drinks
and papers.

Post Office (set in a tiny shed at Brogaig, near the Village Stores)

Oystercatcher Café (open during the summer season serving lunches, teas,
evening meals)

Columba 1400 (café serving lunches, coffees and evening meals, check opening
times on website) www.columba1400.co.uk

Winter view to the Torridon peaks from Flodigarry

STAGE 2
Flodigarry to the Storr

Start	Flodigarry Hostel (NG 464 719)
Finish	Storr car park on A855 (NG 508 529)
Distance	28.5km (17¾ miles)
Total Ascent	1750m
Time	8½–10hrs
Terrain	Tough hillwalking, pathless in places and requiring good navigation skills especially in poor weather
Maps	Harvey – The Skye Trail; OS Explorer 408 Trotternish

This is the most challenging stage of the Skye Trail as it climbs from Flodigarry through the astonishing rock formations of The Quiraing before heading up onto the great escarpment that is the Trotternish Ridge. Often rated as one of the best ridgewalks in Britain, the tough going is rewarded by fabulous views. However, it should be borne in mind that the route is long, very exposed to the elements and difficult to navigate on in poor conditions. There are very few escape routes so do consider alternatives if the forecast is poor and be sure to carry a map. A route profile is included to give you an idea of what you are facing.

The stage ends at the A855 Storr car park where there is a bus stop nearby for buses to Staffin or Portree if you complete the walk in time. Alternatively, you may be able to arrange a pick-up from some B&Bs or taxi, but do not depend on getting a reliable mobile phone signal.

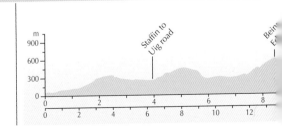

Looking back to the Quiraing

If you have spent the night at Dun Flodigarry Hostel head up the driveway and turn left to follow the road south for a short distance to reach a footpath signed for Loch Langaig on the right. If you are returning from Staffin on the bus, ask the driver to drop you at the layby here and follow the path through the gate. Loch Langaig is soon succeeded by Loch Hasco, with great views back out over Flodigarry Island (Eilean Flodigarry) and across to the peaks of Torridon on the mainland. Continue following the clear path uphill; when you are below the towering cliffs of the **Quiraing** bear left onto a footpath which cuts across the slopes beneath the dramatic crags, eventually climbing a stile at a fence and passing beneath a large overhang. ▶

As the path climbs you will pass the triple summit of **The Prison** on the left, which is reserved for seasoned scramblers, while to the right the pinnacle known as **The Needle** comes into view. From here the path descends

This is the heart of the Quiraing, a crazy world of cliffs and pinnacles.

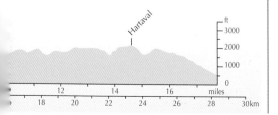

55

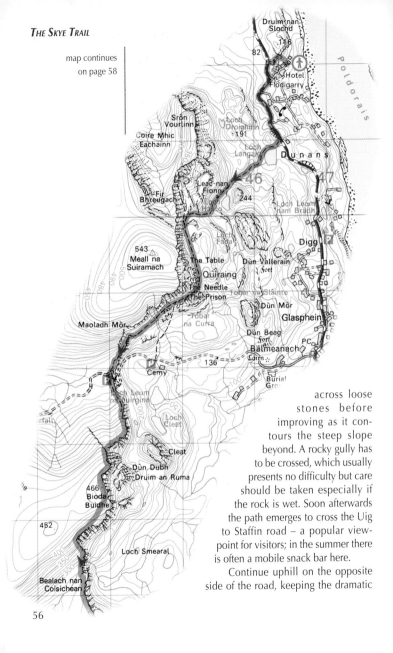

map continues
on page 58

across loose
stones before
improving as it con-
tours the steep slope
beyond. A rocky gully has
to be crossed, which usually
presents no difficulty but care
should be taken especially if
the rock is wet. Soon afterwards
the path emerges to cross the Uig
to Staffin road – a popular viewpoint for visitors; in the summer there
is often a mobile snack bar here.

Continue uphill on the opposite
side of the road, keeping the dramatic

edge of the ridge on your left on the climb to a false summit on a grassy platform. A short descent precedes a final pull up to the summit of **Bioda Buidhe** at 466m. Immediately below is a chaos of landslides and pinnacles, backed by Staffin Bay with its clear crofting strips set out running down to the shore. The ridge is also a good vantage point for watching both golden and white-tailed eagles taking advantage of the thermals. These giant raptors are sometimes seen circling below the top of the cliffs so you have the chance to look down on them rather than craning skywards.

In poor visibility careful navigation is needed on the steep descent to **Bealach Uige**, from where the long, steady climb ahead up the flank of **Beinn Edra** begins. The summit at 611m does not come into view until the last moment – a great and little-visited viewpoint at the heart of the peninsula.

TROTTERNISH DINOSAURS

Walking through the weird rock formation of Trotternish, it's not hard to imagine that 175 million years ago dinosaurs roamed the landscape. Remarkable fossil finds from the Jurassic period have confirmed that both herbivorous and carnivorous dinosaurs lived here. The pebble foreshore at Flodigarry is a good place to pick up belemnites, the cigarette-shaped fossils from ancient squid-like creatures whose external skeletons form the basis for the fossil shapes found today. Much larger and more exciting discoveries have been found at the sandy beach at An Corran on the way to Staffin slipway and at Bearreraig Bay, passed near the start of Stage 3.

At Staffin the footprints can still be seen of a group of ornithopods, herbivorous dinosaurs which walked upright on their hind legs. The footprints are often covered by sand, but at low tide and particularly in winter they are sometimes visible just to the right after you descend the ramp to the beach. Casts of the prints, along with a fascinating collection of other local discoveries, can be found in Staffin Museum, situated on the main A855 road at Ellishadder just south of Staffin.

Evidence of carnivorous dinosaurs, megalosaurus and the omnivorous cetiosaurus and stegosaurus have been found along the coast near Bearreraig Bay, which is a good spot for looking for a range of fossils.

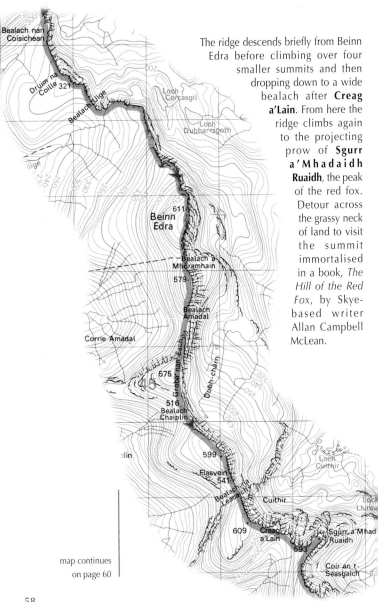

The ridge descends briefly from Beinn Edra before climbing over four smaller summits and then dropping down to a wide bealach after **Creag a'Lain**. From here the ridge climbs again to the projecting prow of **Sgurr a'Mhadaidh Ruaidh**, the peak of the red fox. Detour across the grassy neck of land to visit the summit immortalised in a book, *The Hill of the Red Fox*, by Skye-based writer Allan Campbell McLean.

Bealach nan Coisichean

Druim na Coille 321

Bealach Uige

Loch Corcasgil

Loch Dubhar-sgoth

611 Beinn Edra

Bealach a Mhoramhain

579

Bealach Amadal

Corrie Amadal

Groban nan Each

Dubh-chàin

575

516 Bealach Chaiplin

599

Flasvein 541

Bealach na Leacaich

Cuithir

Loch Cuithir

609 Creag a'Lain

593

Sgurr a'Mhad Ruaidh

Coir an t-Seasgaich

map continues on page 60

From the top of Sgurr a'Mhadaidh Ruaidh you can look down to see evidence of an intriguing story from Skye's industrial past. Loch Cuithir lies directly below and you should be able to make out the straight lines of an **old railway** that once transported diatomite, a soft sedimentary rock extracted from the bed of the loch, to the coast at Lealt where it was dried in kilns to be exported for use in a wide variety of materials, ranging from toothpaste to gunpowder.

When it began in 1899 the railway was powered by gravity and human effort, but was later steam driven. A similar enterprise ran in nearby Staffin where an aerial ropeway was used to transport the clay-like substance to the sea – in one notable incident a failure of the ropeway caused the demolition of a house.

At its peak the Skye Diatomite Company employed over 50 people. Until the road around the Trotternish peninsula was built in the 1950s the sea was the only form of transport. It was actually the arrival of the road which led to the decline of

Sgurr a'Mhadaidh Ruadh

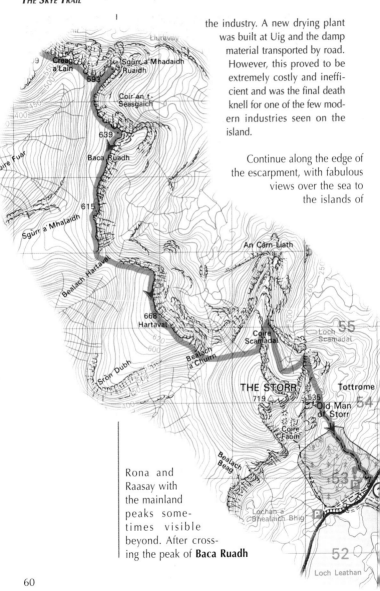

the industry. A new drying plant was built at Uig and the damp material transported by road. However, this proved to be extremely costly and inefficient and was the final death knell for one of the few modern industries seen on the island.

Continue along the edge of the escarpment, with fabulous views over the sea to the islands of Rona and Raasay with the mainland peaks sometimes visible beyond. After crossing the peak of **Baca Ruadh**

the ridge undulates until dropping steeply down a rocky slope to **Bealach Hartaval**. A short sharp climb brings you to an easier section before the summit of **Hartaval** (668m) is reached. The route next descends, skirting a few rocky outcrops, to the **Bealach a'Chuin**, at the foot of the Storr.

▶ First continue slightly north of east to reach the ridge leading up to the Storr summit (if you are feeling energetic you can continue up to the top of the Storr before returning to this point). Aim north down this ridge until it is possible to descend a grassy section of the slope on the right to meet a path coming up from the cliffs of the Storr. Now follow this path to the right traversing round the grassy bowl of the upper corrie. A short rocky downward scramble has to be negotiated at the far end of **Coire Scamadal** – normally it presents no problems but care should be taken especially in wet weather. The path now leads to a stile over a fence and once over this the famous image of the Old Man of Storr and the Needle with the backdrop of the Storr Lochs comes into view. Although it may be familiar from countless photographs and calendars, this image still takes your breath away.

Old Man of Storr and the Storr cliffs

Careful navigation is needed here.

Rubha Sùghar

Bearreraig Bay

Below the cliffs of the Storr

Pick up the large, clear path and descend southwards, passing to the left of the Needle, and then the great pinnacle of the **Old Man of Storr** himself. For the first time since the Quiraing you are likely to find yourself among other walkers – the Storr is always busy whatever the weather. A path leads downhill to a gate and then descends through an area of recently felled forestry which will eventually be partially replanted with native trees. The path emerges onto the road at a car park but there are no facilities here; the bus stop for Portree is just a short way to the right on the far side of the road, or you could arrange for a pick up by taxi.

STORR

Accommodation providers (there is a range of them) in Staffin or Portree may be able to pick you up from here by arrangement and by doing this you could spend two nights in the same accommodation. Alternatively if you complete the walk fast enough you may be able to pick up the bus to either Staffin or Portree and then get the same bus back in the morning. The Glenview hotel 9.5km north at Culnacnoc serves a delicious range of local produce and would be a luxurious haven after this tough day, but bus, taxi or other transport would still need to be arranged. Wild camping possibilities are probably best found before you descend to the road, although if you have the energy and the weather is up to it, a wild camp down on the foreshore at Bearreraig Bay could provide an atmospheric night.

Accommodation and Facilities

The Glenview (stylish boutique hotel serving great local food; you would need to arrange transport from the end of the stage)
www.glenviewskye.co.uk 01470 562248

Beinn Edra House B&B and Self-Catering www.valtosskye.co.uk 01470 562461

STAGE 3

Storr to Portree via the coastline

Start	Storr car park (NG 508 529)
Finish	Portree (NG 482 436)
Distance	14km (8¾ miles)
Total Ascent	510m
Time	5–6hrs
Terrain	Pathless, boggy and rough for the first 3km after leaving the road after which the terrain improves. Some steep sections and always near unfenced high cliffs
Maps	Harvey – The Skye Trail; OS Explorer 410 Portree

Leaving the Trotternish Ridge behind, the third day of the Skye Trail takes to the coast once more, crossing rough and pathless moorland above dramatic cliffs with breathtaking views. If you have plenty of time and the weather is fair you can include a detour via a steep descent to Bearreraig Bay, a perfect arc of pebbly shore favoured by fossil hunters and also good for a spot of otter watching. The stage ends at Portree, the main village on the island. Portree makes a great base for a rest day with plenty of places of interest accessible by bus, boat trips to view sea eagles during the summer season, and a range of eating and re-stocking opportunities.

The square flat roofed building is the winch house which is used to pull a carriage up and down a funicular track to the hydro station below.

From the Storr car park head south along the A855 towards Portree for a very short distance. Take the minor road branching off to the left near the bus stop to head towards the coast. The road crosses the damn and out-flow of Loch Leathan, one of the Storr Lochs, popular fishing lochs which have been harnessed for hydro electric power. After crossing the dam continue along the road and turn right to leave the road at a path sign to follow a short section of path skirting the house and turning area. ◄

The main walk turns right at a Scotways sign but before heading that way detour left to a viewpoint overlooking **Bearreraig Bay** – the site of the hydro-power station.

Road to the cottage above Bearreraig Bay

It is possible to visit **Bearreraig Bay** by following a steep zig-zag path down to the shore where you can pass in front of the tiny power station, the first to bring electricity to the island in the 1950s – however, don't underestimate the climb back up! One hundred and seventy million years ago this area was home to a number of dinosaurs, and remains of plesiosaurs and other creatures have been found here, but you are more likely to find ammonites and belemnites.

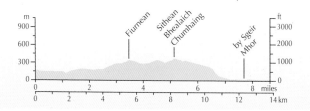

65

Cliffs above Bearreraig Bay

FLORA MACDONALD AND THE PRINCE'S FLIGHT

Flora MacDonald was born on South Uist although she was raised at Armadale in Sleat. In 1746 she was living in Benbecula when the fleeing Prince Charles arrived, seeking refuge and a safe hiding place. She disguised the Prince as her maid Betty Burke, and they were rowed across the Minch with a crew of six, landing at what is now known as Prince Charles' Point in Trotternish, a couple of miles north of Uig.

They hid there in a cottage before making a clandestine overland journey to Portree together. Here they parted, and Charles gave Flora a locket with his portrait and promised they would meet again. Charles hid for a time on Raasay but his flight continued with a gruelling night march from Portree to Elgol. They crossed the moors to Sligachan before passing over the Red Hills just north of Marsco, then headed through Strath Mor to reach Elgol where Charles stayed overnight in a cave before taking another boat for the mainland. He eventually made it back to France, sailing from Arisaig on 20 September 1746.

Flora MacDonald was arrested and brought to London for trial. She was imprisoned in the Tower of London, and was for a time under sentence of death, but was released in 1747. Afterwards, she emigrated to America, and tried to recruit Scots living there to support the British government during the War of Independence. Later she returned to live in Skye, at Kingsburgh in Trotternish and at Flodigarry. In later life she was something of a celebrity, and she hosted Johnson and Boswell during their tour of the Hebrides. Her grave can be visited at Kilmuir; a monument there bears Johnston's tribute: 'Her name will be mentioned in history, and if courage and fidelity be virtues, mentioned with honour.'

To continue the coastal route, head south from the Scotways sign, crossing boggy moorland at first, aiming directly for the top of a small hillock marked with a wooden post. Keep heading south, staying on the highest ground to avoid the worst of the bogs. When this grassy crest comes to an end aim straight across the moor to a gully seen as a break in the cliffs ahead. Climb this to reach much easier going above. ▶

The islands of Raasay and Rona can be seen clearly and on a good day you can make out the peaks of Torridon on the mainland beyond.

Springy turf is now your reward for the 3km of bog slogging, and the clifftop walk continues over the summit of **Fiurnean** before crossing a col and heading up to **Craig Ulatota**. The next summit is **Sithean Bhealaich Chumhaing**, marked with a trig point and at 392m the highest point of the stage. On a good day you will get your first distant peek at the Cuillin from here. Continue south. At **Rubha na h-Airde Glaise** the escarpment turns southwest, finally ending at Creag Mhor from where Ben Tianavaig can be seen across the waters that form the entrance to **Portree Bay**.

It is not possible to descend directly to the green fields below, so first aim right and descend to reach a post and wire fence, following this downhill keeping well away from the cliff edge. When the fence is joined by another follow this to the left, staying close to the stream as you descend.

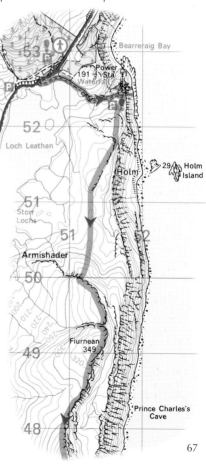

map continues on page 68

The relatively level ground of Bile Pastures will come as a relief. Aim across these using the gates in the fences.

At the stone wall turn left to reach a small wooden gate (out of sight at first – don't be tempted to climb the wall). This leads onto a coastal path (ignore the path heading uphill) which is part of a popular local walk, passing **Sgeir Mhòr**, also known as Black Rock. After reaching a viewpoint and then the sailing club the path emerges onto Scorrybreck Road. Stay ahead on this to cross a river and head up to the A855. Turn left (turn right for the campsite) at this junction to follow Bosville Terrace, which has an excellent outlook over the harbour and a couple of B&Bs, to reach the centre of Portree, passing a small Co-op supermarket on the way.

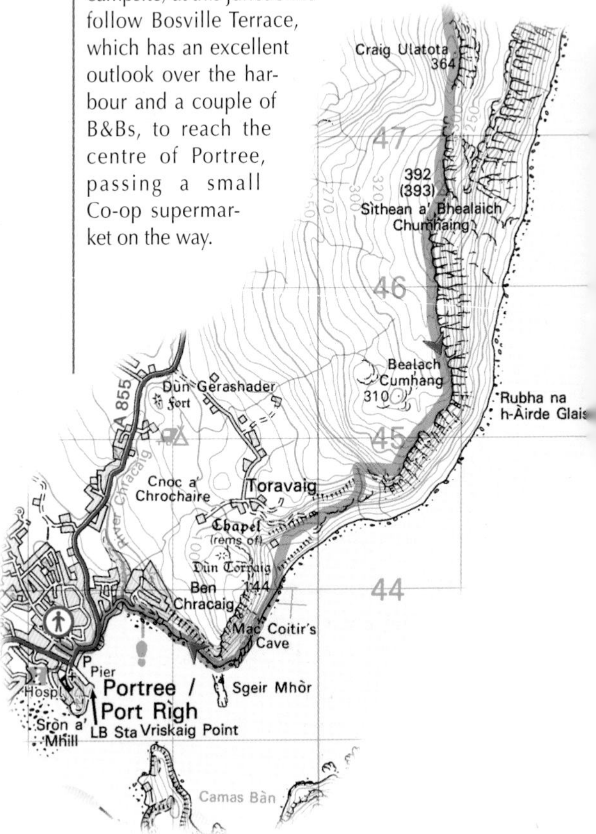

Craig Ulatota
364

47

392
(393)
Sìthean a' Bhealaich
Chumhaing

46

Bealach
Cumhang
310

Rubha na
h-Àirde Glais

Dùn Gerashader
Fort

855

Cnoc a'
Chrochaire

Toravaig

45

Chapel
(rems of)

Dùn Torvaig

Ben
Chracaig

144

44

Mac Coitir's
Cave

Pier

Hosp¹

Portree /
Port Rìgh

Sgeir Mhòr

Sròn a'
Mhill

LB Sta

Vriskaig Point

Camas Bàn

PORTREE

Portree harbour

Portree is the hub of island life and has a number of useful shops, including Inside Out, an outdoor gear shop situated on the misleadingly named Green, (near the Royal Hotel), a chemist, three banks and food shops. Café Arriba has great views overlooking the harbour and brews Skye's best coffee, while the Caledonian Café serves hearty breakfasts, quality traditional meals and good ice cream. The Isles Inn is recommended for pub food and live music; you could also check out what's on at the Gathering Hall near the harbour. There are regular concerts and films at the Aros Centre on the southern edge of the village. If you can keep the hungry seagulls away, the harbour makes a great spot for eating fish and chips from the nearby chippers, and a number of restaurants serve seafood of the non-battered variety. The swimming pool at the Fingal Centre at the High School is open to the public and there is also a library here with internet access. Accommodation options cater for all tastes and budgets, including the brightly coloured Portree Independent Hostel in the centre of the village and the excellent Torvaig Campsite, a 1km hike back up the Staffin road.

Accommodation and Facilities

Portree Independent Hostel www.hostelskye.co.uk 01478 613737

Torvaig Campsite (open Apr–Oct) www.portreecampsite.co.uk 01478 611849

No 5 Bed & Breakfast www.skyeaccommodation-portree.co.uk 01478 612509

Conusg B&B www.conusg.com (email via website)

Meadowbank House B&B www.meadowbankguesthouse.co.uk 01478 612059

Ben Tianavaig B&B (overlooking the harbour and run by keen walkers) www.ben-tianavaig.co.uk 01478 612152

Tarven B&B and Self-Catering www.tarvencottage.com 01478 612679

Viewfield House (characterful country house hotel) www.viewfieldhouse.com 01478 612217

The Royal Hotel www.royal-hotel-skye.com 01478 612525

The Isles Inn (decent pub food and sometimes live music) www.accommodationskye.co.uk 01478 612129

Inside Out (walking and outdoor gear shop) shop.insideoutskye.com 01478 611663

STAGE 4
Portree to Sligachan

Start	Portree (NG 482 436)
Finish	Sligachan Hotel (NG 484 299)
Distance	19km (11¾ miles)
Total Ascent	275m
Time	5–6hrs
Terrain	Minor road, rough path along Loch Sligachan with river crossings which can become impassable after heavy rain
Maps	Harvey – The Skye Trail; OS Explorer 410 Portree

The fourth stage of the Skye Trail starts by skirting the salt marsh at the edge of Portree Bay before taking to the tarmac – thankfully a narrow, quiet ribbon winding its way through the fine scenery and small crofting settlements of the Braes. The final section follows a rough path along the shores of Loch Sligachan, with views to the Red Hills and the Black Cuillin. The stage ends at Sligachan. If you want to add more challenge to the day, the ascent of Ben Tianavaig provides a fantastic 3hr detour which gives excellent views back over much of the route covered so far and is a haunt of golden eagles and sea eagles.

From Portree head out along the main A855 road towards Broadford, ignoring the right turn towards Dunvegan and passing the High School. This section of Viewfield Road is home to many of Portree's numerous B&Bs.

> The last building on the right-hand side after the petrol station and cemetery is the **Aros Centre**. As well as being an arts venue and café this houses exhibitions on Skye and sea eagles, with a live CCTV feed from a nearby nest during the nesting season.

Just before reaching the **Aros Centre**, take a faint path leading down to the shore on the left, which leaves from the far end of the layby between the cemetery and

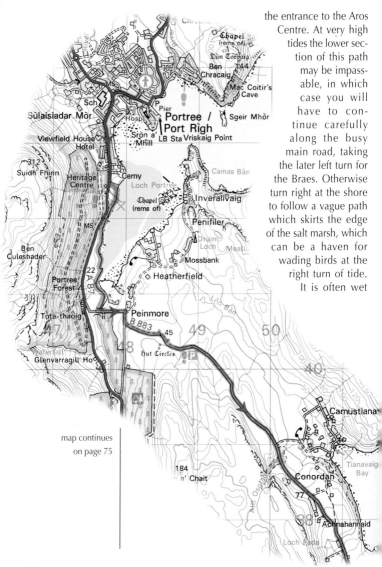

the entrance to the Aros Centre. At very high tides the lower section of this path may be impassable, in which case you will have to continue carefully along the busy main road, taking the later left turn for the Braes. Otherwise turn right at the shore to follow a vague path which skirts the edge of the salt marsh, which can be a haven for wading birds at the right turn of tide. It is often wet

map continues on page 75

underfoot in places although you should be able to pick a route through the marshy area to keep as dry as possible.

On the banks of the Varrigill River

The path follows the Varrigill River for a short distance to reach a gate at the road. Turn left and follow the road uphill, ignoring the turning for Penifiler. The road turns sharp right and then left where another road branches off to the right. Continue as the road undulates and pass the turning for Camustianavaig. ▶

> The **Braes** make up one of the more sheltered parts of Skye which, aside from the Sleat peninsula, is often battered by storms coming straight off the Atlantic. Facing east to Raasay and sheltered by Ben Lee, the townships here are a relative oasis, as the small areas of woodland show.

Pass the community hall, soon reaching the **memorial** to the Battle of the Braes.

> This stone cairn commemorates a significant moment in the struggle for land rights for the people

You could detour here to climb the delightful Ben Tianavaig from the bay; however, this would add an extra 3 to 4hrs to your day and may be best left as a short day walk another time.

of Skye and the Highlands – the **Battles of the Braes**. The memorial reads, 'Near this cairn on 19 April 1882 ended the battle fought by the people of Braes on behalf of the crofters of Gaeldom.' (The full story of the crofters' fight for fair and secure tenancies is told in 'The crofters' struggle' in the Introduction.)

When a junction is reached take the left branch for the best sea views – the two roads join up again at Peinachorran. If time allows you can detour on a path to the left from the red post box to visit one of Skye's rare sandy beaches sweeping round to An Aird. The coastline beyond the beach is also worth exploring, with nesting seabirds, peppered with natural arches and with good views across the Sound to Raasay. Continuing on the road, it climbs to a T-junction – turn left to pass the houses of **Peinachorran**.

At the end of the road there is a signpost for Sligachan; from here gain height on the first section and you'll soon find a better path at a slightly higher level. There are great views across the water to the pier at Sconser where the ferry to Raasay plies back and forth. The path soon

Peinachorran and Glamaig

descends to a large cairn on the shore from where it climbs again to stay at about the same level as it skirts the loch. The route crosses several small burns, the first of which is wooded above the path and has a fine waterfall.

The route continues for about 3km in a similar fashion.

Across the water **Glamaig** looks impressive, its steep northern slopes of broken rock and scree looking quite unassailable. It seems almost unbelievable that the record for the Glamaig Hill Race, a there-and-back challenge from Sligachan, is a mere 44 minutes and 27 seconds.

The view of the Cuillin ahead improves with every step and on a clear day fun can be had identifying the various peaks. Eventually the steep slopes on the right relent and

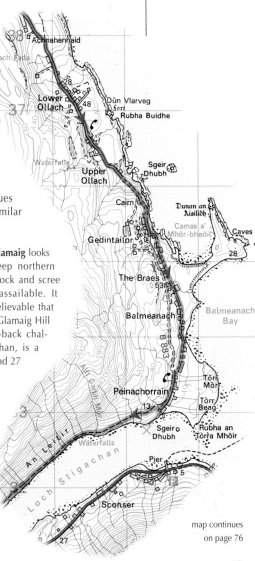

map continues on page 76

75

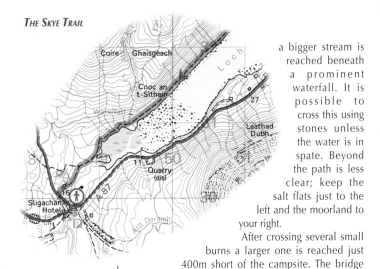

a bigger stream is reached beneath a prominent waterfall. It is possible to cross this using stones unless the water is in spate. Beyond the path is less clear; keep the salt flats just to the left and the moorland to your right.

After crossing several small burns a larger one is reached just 400m short of the campsite. The bridge marked on some OS maps here is a figment of the mapmaker's imagination. There are stones to aid a crossing but these may be covered, in which case it is better to cross slightly to the left where the water is shallowest.

Approaching the Cuillin

Once across the path soon reaches **Sligachan campsite**. Continue to reach the main road and the hotel – the bunkhouse is just a little bit further on past the old stone bridge.

The Sligachan Hotel

SLIGACHAN

Sligachan has a hotel and walker-friendly bar, campsite and nearby separate bunkhouse. As well as serving meals and an enviable selection of single malts, the hotel also has a micro brewery. No reservations are necessary at the campsite, which also has laundry facilities. There is a bus stop here with connections to Portree, Broadford and the mainland.

Accommodation and facilities

Sligachan Hotel & Campsite www.sligachan.co.uk 01478 650204

Sligachan Bunkhouse (sleeps 20 in 4 dorms; free WiFi)
www.sligachanselfcatering.co.uk 01478 650458

STAGE 5
Sligachan to Elgol

Start	Sligachan (NG 484 299)
Finish	Elgol (NG 518 135)
Distance	18km (11¼ miles)
Total Ascent	310m
Time	6–8hrs
Terrain	Rough path with stream crossings to Camasunary, then eroded clifftop path with steep drops. Great care needed
Maps	Harvey – The Skye Trail; OS Explorer 411 Cuillin Hills

The fifth day of the Skye Trail follows dramatic Glen Sligachan, a great trench dividing the forbidding mountain ranges of the Red and Black Cuillin, to reach the beautiful bay at Camasunary. From here the main route follows a vertiginous cliff path to reach the small settlement of Elgol. Classic views across the water to the main Cuillin ridge are your reward for the sometimes awkward path. As the jumping off point for boat trips to Loch Coruisk at the heart of the Cuillin, Elgol is another possible place to have a rest day, especially in good weather. An alternative route (Stage 6B) assumes you will spend a night at Camasunary (either wild camping or in the MBA bothy) before climbing Bla Bheinn the following day via the south ridge to descend to Torrin where the main route is rejoined.

Leave the Sligachan Hotel, crossing the Dunvegan road to take the track over the old stone bridge, built by Thomas Telford and foreground to so many photos of the Cuillin. On the far side take the path which turns off to the right. After a gate in a fence continue straight ahead on a well-made pitched path.

As the route continues up Glen Sligachan you can appreciate the majesty of the **Cuillin** – Britain's rockiest, steepest and trickiest mountain range. There are fine views of Sgurr nan Gillean to the right, with the Red Hills and Marsco to the left.

The Red Hills from Sligachan

map continues on page 81

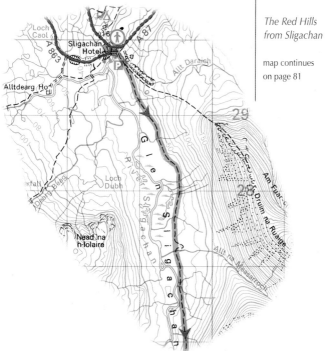

Heading up Glen Sligachan

Underfoot the route becomes gradually rougher as the path crosses numerous small burns, until after about 3km it reaches the larger **Allt na Measarroch**. This is usually straightforward to cross using stones, after which the path passes through a boggy area before becoming drier underfoot on the 3km gradual climb to the watershed. Here two lochans can be seen to the right, and a short distance further on the path forks at a large cairn. ◄

The right fork heads up towards Sgurr na Stri, a fantastic viewpoint but too long a detour for those intending to reach Elgol on foot in a day.

The Skye Trail keeps left to continue down the glen, with imposing views of the west face of Bla Bheinn (often known simply as Blaven) dominating the view. During the late autumn months this is a good place to spot and hear rutting deer, an impressive roaring that can give wild campers a sleepness night. After passing **Loch an Athain** and then the much larger **Loch na Creitheach**, keep on the lower path near the loch. Eventually the flat grassy sward in front of the bay at **Camasunary** is reached.

The house at the east side of the bay is private but the **bothy on the west side** is maintained by the Mountain Bothy Association (MBA) and is a lovely place to spend the night. It remained open in 2014

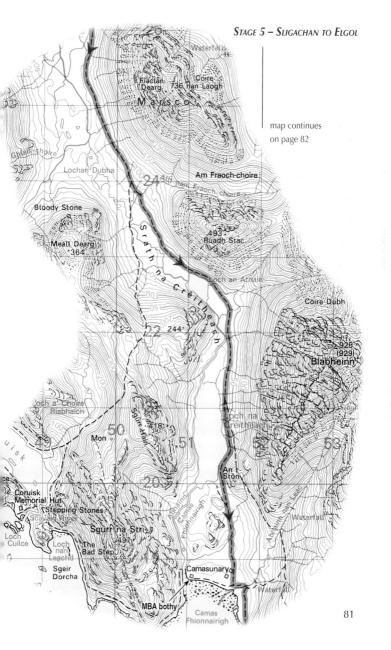

map continues
on page 82

Waterfalls

Fiaclan
Dearg 736 nan Laogh
M a r s c o

Coire
nan Laogh

Ghiallchoire

Lochan Dubha

Am Fraoch-choire

Allt nan Fraoch-choire

Srath na Creitheach

Bloody Stone

Meall Dearg
364

493
Ruadh Stac

Loch an Athain

Coire Dubh

928
(929)
Blabheinn

22 244

Loch a Choire
Riabhaich

50
Mon

Sgurr Hain
418

51

Loch na
Creitheach

52 53

uisk

49

20

An t
Stron

Coruisk
Memorial Hut

Stepping Stones

Scavaig River

Sgurr na Stri
497

Abhainn
Camas
Fhionnairigh

Waterfall

Abhainn nan Leac

Loch
Cuilce

Loch
nan Leachd

The Bad Step

Sgeir
Dorcha

Camasunary

Waterfall

MBA bothy

Camas
Fhionnairigh

81

but its future as a walkers' bothy is uncertain – it may close in the next few years. Check on the Mountain Bothy Association website (**www.mountainbothies. org.uk**) before starting out if you plan to stay here. Otherwise the bay makes a fine wild camping spot.

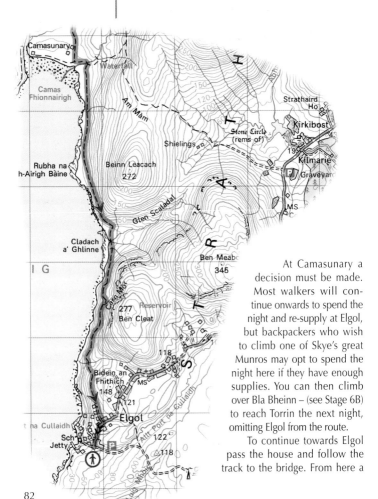

At Camasunary a decision must be made. Most walkers will continue onwards to spend the night and re-supply at Elgol, but backpackers who wish to climb one of Skye's great Munros may opt to spend the night here if they have enough supplies. You can then climb over Bla Bheinn – (see Stage 6B) to reach Torrin the next night, omitting Elgol from the route.

To continue towards Elgol pass the house and follow the track to the bridge. From here a

COLLIE AND MACKENZIE

The early history of climbing and exploration in the Cuillin is forever associated with two men, Norman Collie and John MacKenzie. The two appeared on the surface to have had little in common – Collie an eminent Victorian scientist, MacKenzie a local crofter who acted as a guide – but they became the firmest of friends and pioneered many first ascents here.

Both have Skye peaks named in their honour, and they are buried together in Struan, but a local campaign is set to have the two men commemorated at Sligachan. New information panels have already been installed, and if the fundraising is successful then a 1½ times life size bronze sculpture of the two men will, in future, make a striking foreground for the classic view of the mountains.

path leads south along the shore, boggy at first but soon becoming drier as it climbs a grassy slope. The next section of path should be treated with care – the path is eroded in places and runs along the edge of some high vertical drops. When not looking at your feet, there are fabulous views over the water of Loch Scavaig to the jagged peaks of the Black Cuillin. The path descends to the bay at the foot of **Glen Scaladal**, which might also make a good choice for a wild camp.

Beyond this another ascent is followed by an exposed stretch before the path leaves the cliff edge for the final easier approach to Elgol. After a gate follow a

Coastal path beyond Camasunary

Reaching the road at Elgol path between two fences and then the lane, passing a house on the left. After another house the lane emerges at the road. Turn right to head downhill through **Elgol**, passing a tea shop on the left.

ELGOL

Elgol has a café, a couple of B&Bs and a restaurant with rooms. From the harbour there are boat trips to Loch Coruisk and out to the Small Isles of Rum, Eigg, Canna and Muck. The public toilets, village hall (where showers and internet are available at certain times) and well-stocked shop are all a short distance along the road signed for Glasnakille off to the left.

Accommodation and Facilities

Rose Croft B&B (open Mar–Oct, in the centre of Elgol)
www.rosecroft-bb-elgol.co.uk 01471 866377

Coruisk House B&B and Restaurant, www.coruiskhouse.com 01471 866330

Rowan Cottage B&B, Glasnakille www.rowancottage-skye.co.uk 01471 866287

Elgol Shop and Post Office (check website for opening hours)
www.isleofskye.net/elgolshop 01471 866329

STAGE 6
Elgol to Torrin

Start	Elgol (NG 518 135)
Finish	Torrin (NG 574 210)
Distance	16.5km (10¼ miles)
Total Ascent	370m
Time	5½–6hrs
Terrain	Good paths, track and minor road
Maps	Harvey – The Skye Trail; OS Explorer 411 Cuillin Hills

This presents relatively straightforward walking. Hugging the coast for much of the way, there are views across the water to the Sleat peninsula as well as the Small Isles of Rum, Eigg, Muck and Canna. After a brief road section a much rougher path leads to the remains of a cleared village before the route descends to rejoin the road around the head of Loch Slapin. The stage ends at the small village of Torrin where there is a popular café and a couple of B&Bs.

Leave Elgol by the Glasnakille road, passing the shop and community hall. The road is usually very quiet – sheep rather than cars often seeming to be the most numerous road users. As the road climbs, the dramatic outlines of the islands of Eigg and Rum come into view. After a transmitter mast the road descends to a junction at the scattered settlement of **Glasnakille**.

map continues on page 86

85

Turn left along the minor road to pass several white-washed croft houses with fine views across to Sleat and the mountains of Knoydart beyond. At the road end continue ahead on a grassy track through woodland alive with birds and wildflowers in spring and summer. Beyond a lonely house the track becomes surfaced and soon passes a few more houses. Turn off the road where it climbs to the left to continue straight ahead – downhill – on a track. Head towards a white house and keep a careful eye out for a stone marker indicating the path to the right just before the garden is reached. This hugs the coast before emerging at another minor road near some cottages.

map continues
on page 88

The road soon heads inland, passing the fine **Kilmarie House** on the left.

The track to Kilmarie

This was once the home of **Iain Anderson** lead singer and legendary flute player of the progressive rock band Jethro Tull. Distrusted at first by many locals, the rock star was a hands-on laird when in residence and was instrumental in setting up a thriving fish farm business that provided much needed employment in the late 1970s and 1980s. He eventually sold the surrounding Strathaird Estate to the conservation charity the John Muir Trust.

Detour to Dun Ringill

The route continues up the road, but a footbridge on the right is the start of an optional detour to visit Dun Ringill, the crumbling ruins of a castle built over an ancient broch or fort. To reach it turn right down the far bank of the stream and then follow a grassy path near the shore for 1km, before retracing your steps back to the road.

Follow the road to reach the B8083 at **Kirkibost** and turn right. After 1.2km and once past a small cottage on the right, look out for a fence running down the edge of a forestry plantation on the left of the road at a small layby. Here you can either go through the gate and follow the rough path between the forestry and the fence – which is very boggy higher up – or keep to the right of the fence and climb a pathless section until the ruins of Keppoch are reached at the top, accessible via a stile.

An early victim of the **Highland Clearances**, when tenants were moved off the land to make way for more profitable and easier to manage sheep, Keppoch was forcibly cleared of its 44 families in 1852 – many being forced to board a ship for Australia.

After exploring this atmospheric spot climb back over the stile and continue along the edge of the forestry and then over open ground on an indistinct path. The path bends right to cross a stream on stepping stones – the path can be easily missed here. However, it soon improves and there are great views of the Red Hills and Torrin across Loch Slapin.

After descending, the path crosses a bridge to reach

the car park for Bla Bheinn, a popular Munro which stands apart from the rest of the Black Cuillin and has a panoramic view of all the main peaks. A right turn brings you to the main road; turn left along it to skirt around the head of **Loch Slapin** and eventually reach **Torrin**.

TORRIN

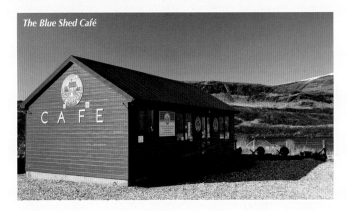
The Blue Shed Café

The salt marsh on the far side is good for a spot of birdwatching or optimistically looking for the elusive otter. There are also a number of potential wild camping pitches before the village is reached. Torrin has two B&Bs and the excellent Blue Shed café, open every day except Wednesday April–October and at weekends in February and March. The bus from Elgol passes through the village on the way to Broadford.

Accommodation and facilities

Skye Mountain Lodge B&B
www.skyemountainlodge.co.uk 01471 822377

A' Chuibheall B&B
www.go-bedandbreakfast.co.uk/achuibheall 01471 822469

Blue Shed Café (check website for opening times)
www.theblueshedcafé.co.uk 01471 822847

STAGE 6B
Bla Bheinn alternative – Camasunary to Torrin

Start	Camasunary (NG 516 186)
Finish	Torrin (NG 574 210)
Distance	11km (7 miles)
Total Ascent	970m
Time	7–8hrs
Terrain	Bla Bheinn involves exceptionally rough and rocky walking, and very careful navigation and experience is required. There is some scrambling between the two summits and the descent involves loose rock and scree
Maps	Harvey – The Skye Trail; OS Explorer 411 Cuillin Hills

This stage will appeal to very experienced hillwalkers who wish to climb one of Skye's major mountain summits as part of the route. The route assumes that the fifth day is ended with a wild camp or bothy stay at Camasunary. This route omits Elgol (a useful re-supply point and a beautiful spot in its own right) but does offer the chance to include one of the Cuillin Munros in the journey. It rejoins the main Skye Trail on the road to Torridon. On a good day the views of the main Cuillin ridge from the summit of Bla Bheinn are unforgettable. A profile is included for this stage so that you can see what you are letting yourself in for.

From Camasunary stay on the rough track as it climbs eastwards from the house towards Am Mam. Leave the track where it zig-zags sharply to the right, instead

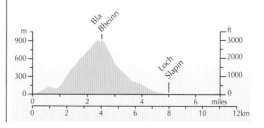

View from the summit of Bla Bheinn

following a path heading northwards. Eventually leave this to head up the south ridge of **Bla Bheinn**. Although very dramatic – and with quite stunning views opening up over Loch Scavaig behind – the ridge leads without any major obstacles all the way to the lower south summit at 926m. The scrambling comes after this, on an awkward descent to the gap between the two summits; this uses a rake on the right (east) flank and requires care. The true sum-mit – at 928m – is reached just beyond.

The descent begins east southeast, never far from vertical cliffs on the left side.

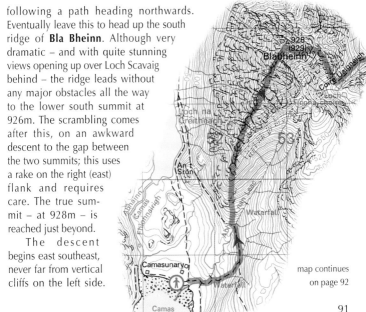

map continues on page 92

91

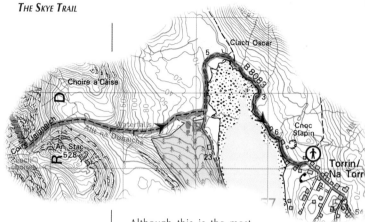

Although this is the most popular route on Bla Bheinn, the rocky ground means that it is mostly without paths. Keep the great cliffs on your left side as the ridge curves northeast. At about 720m the route leaves the ridge and descends a stony gully to the right. This leads down to Fionna-choire and thankfully easier terrain.

From here a clear path heads northeast down the left side of **Coire Uaigneich** and then on down to eventually reach the B8083 road. Turn left for a final road walk around the edge of **Loch Slapin** to **Torrin**.

TORRIN

Torrin has a café (restricted opening in the winter and closed Wednesdays) and two B&Bs. Wild camping spots can be found either side of the village. (See Stage 6 for more information.)

Accommodation and facilities

Skye Mountain Lodge B&B www.skyemountainlodge.co.uk 01471 822377

A' Chuibheall B&B www.go-bedandbreakfast.co.uk/achuibheall 01471 822469

Blue Shed Café www.theblueshedcafé.co.uk 01471 822847

STAGE 7
Torrin to Broadford

Start	Torrin (NG 574 210)
Finish	Broadford (NG 642 235)
Distance	20km (12½ miles)
Total Ascent	480m
Time	6½–7hrs
Terrain	Good paths, track and minor road
Maps	Harvey – The Skye Trail; OS Explorer 412 Sleat

The final stage of the Skye Trail follows the coastline through the atmospheric cleared villages of Suisnish and Boreraig where sheep now wander among the ruined houses. The path runs close to the water at times and there is the added chance that you may spot otters, or more likely seals and numerous seabirds, as you meander along Loch Eishort. The route turns inland from Boreraig to eventually pick up the remains of the Skye Marble Line, a light railway used to transport marble quarried at Torrin to awaiting boats at the quay in Broadford. This larger village has a full range of services and plenty of places to celebrate completing the Skye Trail.

Leave Torrin on the road heading towards Broadford, soon passing the quarry on your right.

map continues
on page 94

Unusually for Skye, the **quarry** sits on a band of limestone which is interspersed with white marble. The quarry deals in both of these, an industry that has continued since the 18th century.

93

Follow the road as it twists and turns before turning right at a junction onto a minor branch which eventually leads down to the shore at **Camas Malag**. This is a delightful spot with neat turf inviting a break while admiring the views of Bla Bheinn across Loch Slapin. A rough track continues southwards along the coast from the road end, heading gently uphill.

After approximately 3km pass through the gate in the fence (an alternative, slightly shorter but rougher path exists on the left-hand side of the fence) towards the remains of **Suisnish**. The only substantial ruins remaining are those of a house which was used more recently by shepherds.

Continue ahead and go through the gate into the enclosure surrounding the metal barn. Turn left, aiming uphill to a gate at the midpoint of the fence at the top of the field. Turn right on the far side of the fence and follow this path through the heather to

map continues on page 97

THE EMPTYING OF SUISNISH

Suisnish was forcibly emptied of its tenants as part of the Highland Clearances in 1853. It gained notoriety because of the witness testimony of geologist Archibald Geikie who was visiting the area at the time. He recalled: 'A strange wailing sound reached my ears, I could see a long and motley procession winding along the road that led north from Suisnish. There were old men and women, too feeble to walk, who were placed in carts; the younger members of the community on foot were carrying their bundles of clothes…while the children, with looks of alarm, walked alongside…. A cry of grief went up to heaven, the long plaintive wail, like a funeral coronach, was resumed…the sound re-echoed through the wide valley of Strath in one prolonged note of desolation.'

eventually descend once more to the shoreline. This part of the trail follows the ancient route linking the two villages of Suisnish and Boreraig. In most parts the path is clear, although in some places small landslips and erosion mean you have to take to the boulders near the sea, which could make the route difficult in stormy conditions. ▶

Look out for a couple of high waterfalls which cascade down the high cliffs.

Looking back from the track to Suisnish

The old coast path

Eventually the more extensive remains of the houses at **Boreraig** are reached. These sit in a fertile and sheltered sward of land but it too suffered at the hands of Lord MacDonald, with all residents being evicted and their homes burnt to make way for sheep. Today it is an atmospheric spot and a place to ponder on the darker side of human nature.

From the ruins look out for a path running up to the right, northeast. The path becomes much clearer as it leaves the ruins behind and climbs with a stream and small valley down to the right. The path crosses moorland before passing through a gate to enter an area that has been planted with native tree species. Soon the path widens to a track and passes a cairn marking the summit of the pass. Ignore the path off to the left and head down to the remains of one of the Skye marble quarries. On the ground a circular structure is all that remains of a winding wheel that once pulled the trains up the incline. Follow the route of the incline downhill, passing spoil heaps.

map continues on page 98

Amid the ruins of Boreraig

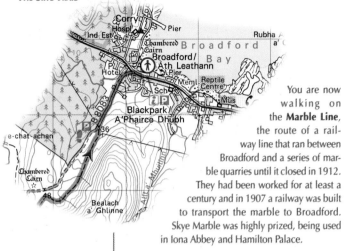

You are now walking on the **Marble Line**, the route of a railway line that ran between Broadford and a series of marble quarries until it closed in 1912. They had been worked for at least a century and in 1907 a railway was built to transport the marble to Broadford. Skye Marble was highly prized, being used in Iona Abbey and Hamilton Palace.

Follow the old railway as it contours along the side of Strath Suardal, passing through two gates above houses at **Suardal** and ignoring any turnings to the left; eventually the path runs alongside the road with a forestry plantation on the far side. At the road turn right through the outskirts of **Broadford**. Look for a short path on the left which heads along the rear of the Broadford Hotel. Alternatively, nip round to the entrance at the front if you fancy celebrating the end of the route with a Drambuie, the recipe for which was allegedly given to the Mackinnons – erstwhile owners of the hotel – by Bonnie Prince Charlie as thanks for providing sanctuary during this flight through Skye. Otherwise continue to the road and turn right to reach the end of the trail and the delights of Broadford.

BROADFORD

Although stretched out along the A855 and slightly blighted by the large Co-op building dominating the shore, Broadford has more than enough facilities to satisfy the tired and hungry walker and the views across the bay are lovely. Some people have even been lucky enough to spot an otter while scoffing their fish and

Beinn na Caillich towers over the town

chips in the shore-side public garden. Both the SYHA hostel and the independent Broadford Backpackers are on the road to the harbour (take the pedestrian bridge), and there are numerous B&Bs, as well as a few hotels, bank, pharmacy, post office and places to eat. City Link coaches stop here on their way to Inverness or Glasgow and local buses ply their way to Kyle of Lochalsh as well as to Portree.

Accommodation & Facilities

Broadford SYHA www.syha.co.uk 01471 822442

Broadford Backpackers www.broadfordbackpackers.co.uk 01471 820333

Hillview B&B www.hillview-skye.co.uk 01471 822 083

Otter Lodge B&B www.otterlodgeskye.co.uk 01471 822954

Tigh an Dochais B&B www.skyebedbreakfast.co.uk 01471 820022

Taigh an Uillt B&B www.b-and-b-broadford.co.uk 01471 822433

Broadford Hotel www.broadfordhotel.co.uk 01471 822204

Hebridean Hotel www.hebrideanhotel.co.uk 01471 822486

Waterfront Takeaway (recommended for fish and chips; open all year, closed Sundays) www.waterfront-takeaway.co.uk

Claymore Restaurant (good bar meals) www.claymore-restaurant-skye.co.uk 01471 822 333

APPENDIX A
Route summary table

Stage	Title	Distance	Total Ascent	Duration	Page
Stage 1	Rubha Hunish to Flodigarry	11.5km (7¼ miles)	290m	5½–6½hrs	44
Stage 2	Flodigarry to The Storr	28.5km (17¾ miles)	1750m	8½–10hrs	54
Stage 3	The Storr to Portree	14km (8¾ miles)	510m	5–6hrs	64
Stage 4	Portree to Sligachan	19km (11¾ miles)	275m	5–6hrs	71
Stage 5	Sligachan to Elgol	18km (11¼ miles)	310m	6–8hrs	78
Stage 6	Elgol to Torrin	16.5km (10¼ miles)	370m	5½–6hrs	85
Stage 6B	Camasunary to Torrin via Bla Bheinn	11km (6¾ miles)	970m	7–8hrs	90
Stage 7	Torrin to Broadford	20km (12½ miles)	480m	6½–7hrs	93
Total (excluding Stage 6B)		**128km (80 miles)**	**3985m**		

Path below the Quiraing (Stage 2)

APPENDIX B
Accommodation

Duntulm area, north Trotternish

Duntulm Castle Hotel
www.duntulmcastle.co.uk
01470 552213

Kilmaluag Bay B&B
www.kilmaluagbay.co.uk

Kilmuir House B&B
www.kilmuir-skye.co.uk
01470 542262

Staffin

Hostels

Dun Flodigarry Hostel
www.hostelflodigarry.co.uk
01470 552212

Bed & Breakfast/Hotels

Achtalean B&B
www.achtalean.co.uk
01470 562723

Bealach Uige B&B
www.skyeaccommodation-staffin.co.uk
01470 562434

Ceol na Mara B&B
www.ceolnamara.co.uk
01470 562242

Dunmar B&B
www.dunmarbandb.co.uk
01470 562411

Gairloch View B&B
www.gairlochview.co.uk
01470 562718

The Flodigarry Hotel
www.hotelintheskye.co.uk
01470 552203

Campsites

Dun Flodigarry Hostel
www.hostelflodigarry.co.uk
01470 552212

Staffin Campsite
www.staffincampsite.co.uk
01470 562213

Self-Catering

Staffin Bay Cottages
www.staffinbaycottages.co.uk
01466 760244

The Old Inn
www.theoldinnstaffin.co.uk

Braeside Cottage
www.staffinselfcatering.co.uk
enquiries@staffinselfcatering.co.uk

Wavecrest
www.wavecrestchalet.co.uk
01786 832119

Island View
www.islandviewskye.com

An Slinnean
www.anslinnean.co.uk
01470 552 392

Cul na Cnoc/Valtos

The Glenview (restaurant with rooms)
www.glenviewskye.co.uk
01470 562248

Beinn Edra House B&B and Self-Catering
www.valtosskye.co.uk
01470 562461

Valtos Croft House (self-catering)
www.croftonskye.co.uk
07748 240882

Portree

Hostels

Portree Independent Hostel
www.hostelskye.co.uk
01478 613737

Bayfield Backpackers
www.skyehostel.co.uk
01478 612231

Bed & Breakfast/Hotels

No 5 Bed & Breakfast
www.skyeaccommodation-portree.co.uk
01478 612509

Conusg B&B
www.conusg.com (email via website)

Meadowbank House B&B
www.meadowbankguesthouse.co.uk
01478 612059

Ben Tianavaig B&B
www.ben-tianavaig.co.uk
01478 612152

Tarven B&B and Self-Catering
www.tarvencottage.com
01478 612679

Viewfield House
www.viewfieldhouse.com
01478 612217

The Royal Hotel
www.royal-hotel-skye.com
01478 612525

The Isles Inn
www.accommodationskye.co.uk
01478 612129

Campsites

Torvaig Campsite, 1km from village
centre on A885 Staffin road
www.portreecampsite.co.uk
01478 611849

Self-Catering

Harbour View – apartment sleeping 3
with stunning views
www.harbourviewportree.co.uk
01471 855253

Portree Bay Cottage – waterside
location, sleeps 6
www.portreebaycottage.co.uk
07703 610396

Camus Ban – centrally located house
sleeping 5
www.camus-ban.co.uk
01456 459347

Skye Holiday Apartments – sleeps 4,
available for short breaks
www.skyeholidayapartments.co.uk
01224 705681

Canopy – luxurious retreat for 2
www.skyeselfcateringcanopy.co.uk
01478 612 766

Sligachan

Sligachan Hotel & Campsite
www.sligachan.co.uk
01478 650204

Sligachan Bunkhouse
www.sligachanselfcatering.co.uk
01478 650458

Elgol

Rose Croft B&B
www.rosecroft-bb-elgol.co.uk
01471 866 377

Coruisk House B&B and Restaurant
www.coruiskhouse.com
014 7186 6330

Glasnakille

Rowan Cottage B&B
www.rowancottage-skye.co.uk
01471 866 287

Torrin

Skye Mountain Lodge B&B
www.skyemountainlodge.co.uk
01471 822377

A' Chuibheall B&B
www.go-bedandbreakfast.co.uk/
achuibheall
01471 822469

Blue Shed Café
www.theblueshedcafé.co.uk
01471 822847

Broadford

Hostels

Broadford SYHA
www.syha.co.uk
01471 822442

Broadford Backpackers
www.broadfordbackpackers.co.uk
01471 820333

B&B/Hotels

Hillview B&B
www.hillview-skye.co.uk
01471 822083

Otter Lodge B&B
www.otterlodgeskye.co.uk
01471 822954

Tigh an Dochais
www.skyebedbreakfast.co.uk
01471 820022

Taigh an Uillt B&B
www.b-and-b-broadford.co.uk
01471 822433

Broadford Hotel
www.broadfordhotel.co.uk
01471 822204

Hebridean Hotel
www.hebrideanhotel.co.uk
01471 822486

Self-Catering

Waterside Cottage
www.watersidecottageskye.co.uk
01471 833708

Fossil Cottage
www.fossil-cottage-skye.co.uk
01471 822 297

Tigh Holm Cottages
www.tigh-holm-cottages.com
01471 820077

Aisling Cottage
www.isleofskyecottage.co.uk
01471 822 297

APPENDIX C
Useful contacts

Skye Trail website
www.skyetrail.org.uk

Inside Out
(outdoor gear shop in Portree)
shop.insideoutskye.com
01478 611663

Coach and buses

Citylink
www.citylink.co.uk

Stagecoach
www.stagecoachbus.com

Taxis

Portree

Dicky's
01478 613388

Gus's
01478 613000

Kenny's
01478 611844

Fastcabs
01478 612200

Broadford

Broadford Private Hire
07972 070891

Hospitals

Portree
01478 613200

Broadford
01471 822491

Mountain Rescue

In an emergency dial 999 or 112 and ask for police, and then mountain rescue.

Baggage transfer and holiday companies

Macs Adventure
www.macsadventure.com

Explore Outdoors
www.explore-outdoors.co.uk

Simply Scotland Tours
www.simplyscotlandtours.co.uk

C-N-Do Scotland
www.cndoscotland.com

Information

Portree Tourist Information Centre, Bayfield House
01478 612137

Highland Council Ranger Service
www.highland.gov.uk/
leisureandtourism/what-to-see/rangers

Mountain Bothies Association
www.mountainbothies.org.uk

Scottish Outdoor Access Code
www.outdooraccess-scotland.com

APPENDIX D
Glossary of Gaelic words

Gaelic	English
abhainn	river
aird	high promontory
airigh	shieling, summer shelter
allt	burn, stream
aros	house
bàgh/bhaigh	bay
baile	town, settlement
ban, bhan	white
beag	small
bealach	pass, col, shoulder
beinn	hill, mountain, peak
beithe	birch tree
bodach	old man
buidhe	yellow
brae	slope
caisteal	castle
camas	channel, creek
caol	narrow area of water, strait
clachan	village
cladh	churchyard
cleit	cliff
cnoc	small hill, knoll
coire	corrie
creag	crag, rock, cliff
dearg	red
deas	south
druim	ridge
dubh	black, dark
dun	fort
ear	east

Gaelic	English
eas	waterfall
eilean	island
fada	long
fank	sheep pen
fasgadh	shelter
froach	heather
fuar	cold
fuaran	spring, well
glas	grey, green
iar	west
iolaire	eagle
lairig	pass, facing slope of hill
leitir	slope
loch	lake
meall	rounded hill
mol	shingle beach
mòr, mhòr	big
mullach	summit
ord	cone shaped hill
ruadh	red
rubha	headland
sgurr, sgorr	peak
strath	valley
stuc	pinnacle, peak
talla	hall (village hall)
tigh, taigh	house
tuath	north
tràigh	beach
uamh, uaimh	cave
uig	bay
uisge	water, rain

APPENDIX E
Further reading

A Long Walk on the Isle of Skye by David Paterson (Peak Publishing 1999). An inspiring read about this pioneering 75-mile south to north route, with excellent photographs.

The Skye Trail by Cameron McNeish and Richard Else (Mountain Media 2010). Hardback book based on the TV programme presented by Cameron McNeish outlining his experience of the Skye Trail, the island and its people.

Hostile Habitats – Scotland's Mountain Environment: A Hillwalkers' Guide to Wildlife and the Landscape by Mark Wrightham and Nick Kempe (Scottish Mountaineering Trust 2006). Hardback book packed full of useful information in a very readable format.

Skye: A Landscape Fashioned by Geology by David Stephenson and John Merritt (Scottish Natural Heritage 1993). One of a series of booklets explaining the mysteries of the geology of Scotland.

Tramping in Skye by R M Humble (Grant and Murray 1993; Pocket Mountains 2010). A fascinating account of Humble's exploration of the island as a young man and enthusiastic walker and climber.

Skye: The Island and its Legends by Otta Swire (Birlinn 2006). Recounts the many myths and legends of Skye folklore going right back to early pre-Christian times.

A Journey to the Western Isle of Scotland Book by Samuel Johnson (1775). An account of Johnson's three-month trip to Scotland with James Boswell in 1773, with fascinating descriptions of the society they found.

A Journal of a Tour to the Hebrides with Samuel Johnson, LL.D. by James Boswell (1785) Published after Johnson's death this is Boswell's diary, which contains an intimate and amusing account of Johnson's antics on the trip. Both Johnson's and Boswell's books are available in a single volume by Penguin Classics or as e-books.

The Isle of Skye: A Walker's Guide by Terry Marsh (Cicerone 2009). A reliable guide to 87 walks and scrambles covering the whole of the island including the Cuillin.

Bla Bheinn and Loch Slapin (Stage 6)

Isle of Skye: 40 Coast and Country Walks by Paul and Helen Webster (Pocket Mountains 2008). Forty shorter walks exploring the whole of the island by the authors of this guide.

A Year in the Life of the Isle of Skye by Bill Birkett (Frances Lincoln 2008). A photographic review of the changing seasons focusing on the Red Cuillin, Black Cuillin and Trotternish.

The Hill of the Red Fox by Allan Campbell McLean (Floris Books 2006). A children's adventure set on Skye during the era of the Cold War.

From Wood to Ridge: Collected Poems by Sorley MacLean (Carcanet Press Ltd 1999). A wonderful collection of poems in both Gaelic and Sorley MacLean's own translation, including Halaig and The Cuillin.

On the Crofters' Trail by David Craig (Birlinn 2006). David Craig sets out to discover the stories of the Highland Clearances which survive in the memories of their descendants.

LISTING OF CICERONE GUIDES

For full information on all our
guides, books and eBooks, visit
our website: **www.cicerone.co.uk**.

Walking – Trekking – Mountaineering – Climbing – Cycling

Over 40 years, Cicerone have built up an outstanding collection of 300 guides, inspiring all sorts of amazing adventures.

 Every guide comes from extensive exploration and research by our expert authors, all with a passion for their subjects. They are frequently praised, endorsed and used by clubs, instructors and outdoor organisations.

All our titles can now be bought as **e-books** and many as iPad and Kindle files and we will continue to make all our guides available for these and many other devices.

Our website shows any **new information** we've received since a book was published. Please do let us know if you find anything has changed, so that we can pass on the latest details. On our **website** you'll also find some great ideas and lots of information, including sample chapters, contents lists, reviews, articles and a photo gallery.

It's easy to keep in touch with what's going on at Cicerone, by getting our monthly **free e-newsletter**, which is full of offers, competitions, up-to-date information and topical articles. You can subscribe on our home page and also follow us on **Facebook** and **Twitter**, as well as our **blog**.

Cicerone – the very best guides for exploring the world.

CICERONE

2 Police Square Milnthorpe Cumbria LA7 7PY
Tel: 015395 62069 info@cicerone.co.uk
www.cicerone.co.uk